WHY WE LOVE BEER

ALL YOU NEED TO KNOW ABOUT BEER HISTORY,
FLAVORS, TYPES OF BEER, AND MORE

KNOWING PLACES NEAR AND FAR
IS NOT WORTH IT; IT IS JUST THEORETICAL;
KNOWING WHERE THE BEST BEER COMES FROM,
IS PRACTICAL, IT IS GEOGRAPHY.

Johann Wolfgang von Goethe

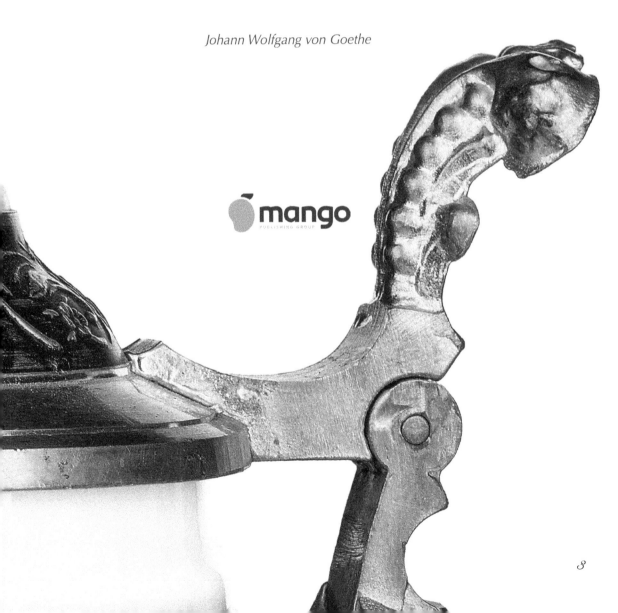

Project editor VALERIA MANFERTO DE FABIANIS

Editorial assistant LAURA ACCOMAZZO

Graphic design MARIA CUCCHI

PHOTOGRAPHS BY FABIO PETRONI

TEXT BY PIETRO FONTANA

RECIPES BY CHEF GIOVANNI RUGGIERI

CONTENTS

WHY WE LOVE BEER

PREFACE

B eer, the oldest and most widely consumed fermented product in the world, is currently experiencing a resurgence in popularity. It has become a global phenomenon, from the United States to Australia, Japan, and throughout Europe. People are increasingly seeking out craft beers in pubs, discussing microbreweries, and savoring beers with extraordinary, unique flavors and enticing aromas.

This phenomenon is characterized by a dual nature: innovation and tradition. The innovation aspect originated in the United States in the late 1970s, while the tradition aspect hails from Great Britain, where CAMRA (the Campaign for Real Ale) enthusiasts are dedicated to reviving the nearly lost Anglo-Saxon brewing tradition.

Microbreweries began proliferating in the United States in the 1970s, and by the late 1990s, small groups of pioneers in other parts of the world started producing their own beers. Belgium saw new breweries emerge alongside existing ones; Scandinavia and Denmark contributed to the microbrewery movement, Italy began crafting artisanal beers, and the Czech Republic, freed from the Iron Curtain, revitalized its brewing traditions. This movement has since spread globally, from north to south and east to west.

While such beers have always existed, they were often taken for granted and forgotten, overshadowed by commercial lagers with their bland colors and flavors. Without denigrating these mass-produced products, it's essential to remember that beer is a living product, capable of stimulating the senses and telling a story. It's the story of the brewer and the land where they grew up and work, and to appreciate it fully, all one needs to do is learn to "listen."

This book serves as an initial step in the journey of understanding the world of brewing. I hope that for you, the passion for beer embodied by Gambrinus will be like a revelation on the road to Damascus. Always keep in mind that beer is the third (or fourth, or fifth...) friend at the table during conversations, perhaps in a cozy pub in the evening. It knows how to gracefully stay in the background without being obtrusive, all while providing immense satisfaction with every sip. And if consumed in moderation, it can enhance the flow of conversation.

Cheers!

Andrea Camaschella

This 16th-century engraving of the English school shows the hop harvest. The female flowers of this sun-loving climber are typically collected in late summer. They are used to give beer its characteristic bitter taste, and a multitude of different aromas (spicy, herbaceous, fruity, citrus and resinous).

THE ORIGINS OF BEER

BEER B.C.

etermining the exact moment beer was first created remains elusive. What we do know is that ever since humans transitioned to agriculture and established settlements, waiting for cereal harvests, they've brewed beer. Discoveries from around 8000 B.C. in Palestine and Jordan, especially in regions like Jericho, Nahal Oren, and Tell Aswad, showcase the first "semi-domesticated" grains—variants selected by farmers and distinct from wild types. It's likely that these or similar grains played a role in the earliest, perhaps accidental, beer creations in human history.

Fermentation processes sprang up independently across millennia and in many world regions: from North America to Mesopotamia and South America to Africa. Evidence points to traditional foods originating from watery cereal broth left to ferment. When writing was invented, the earliest mention of beer, from approximately 4000 B.C., came from the Sumerians in Mesopotamia. Tablets and bas-reliefs described a drink made from barley, baked bread, and water termed "kas," which translates to "that which the mouth desires." Typically crafted by women and sometimes infused with dates or honey, this beverage was consumed from large communal containers. People drank together using long straws, similar to those unearthed in the royal cemetery of Ur. Sumerian beer was often part of workers' wages and held sacred significance, especially for the goddess Ninkasi, as hymns to her attest. Since its debut in written human history, beer has been cherished both as a valuable asset and a means of fostering camaraderie.

The subsequent Mesopotamian civilization, the Babylonians, left numerous traces of beer's role in daily life. The first documented legal code, the Code of Hammurabi, even set forth laws about beer! Specifically, the code mandated daily beer distribution to citizens based on social standing. Unauthorized sale or dilution of beer invited a death penalty. Later discoveries indicate around twenty beer varieties—from pale "liquid bread" to rich, flavored dark types—were available in Babylonian markets. Beer was also a staple at funeral rituals, where it was a communal drink. Ancient Egypt revered beer as a staple drink. Diluted with water and honey, it was even administered to infants during weaning or if breast milk was insufficient. Numerous papyri outline beer-based medicinal recipes; the renowned Ebers Papyrus alone lists over six hundred. Viewed as genuine nourishment, beer, especially the high-alcohol versions made from malt and flavored with hops, juniper, ginger, etc., was a significant part of pyramid builders' diets. During Pharaoh Ramesses II's era, beer production was standardized, and scribes added a new hieroglyph symbolizing an enduring craft: the master brewer.

In the sacred Hebrew scriptures, the Bible and the Talmud, beer is referenced multiple times. It's the drink of choice during the Feast of Unleavened Bread, which commemorates the escape from Egypt, and also during the Feast of Purim. In ancient Greece, folks primarily drank beer during celebrations honoring Demeter, the goddess of harvest and grain. This was also the case during the Olympiads, when drinking wine was prohibited. On the Italian peninsula, before the Romans, the Etruscans had already been consuming "pevakh," a beverage initially crafted from spelt and rye, but later made from wheat, typically sweetened with honey. In Celtic lore, the hero Mag Meld founded the Irish nation, drawing strength from a beer recipe he pilfered from the mythical forest-dwelling Fomorians. In Germanic culture, the earliest historical evidence tied to beer dates back to 800 B.C., marked by a beer amphora found near Kulmbach.

The Romans, although predominantly wine drinkers, gradually warmed up to beer, especially after interacting with the Gauls and Germanic tribes. In fact, beer was the primary alcoholic beverage in regions inhabited by the Celtic and Germanic tribes. This was because the cooler climates of Northern Europe weren't conducive to vine growth, although that's changed recently due to climate change. When Gnaeus Julius Agricola, the governor of Britain, came back to Rome after his military endeavors, he wasn't alone. He brought along three master brewers from Glevum (modern-day Gloucester) so he could craft for himself, and the more adventurous Romans, the drink he'd grown fond of during his time overseas!

BEER A.D.

In the first centuries A.D., Imperial Rome knew and appreciated beer, albeit as an "exotic" product. There is evidence that Nero received gifts of beer from the Iberian Peninsula, and he even had a Portuguese slave at his court whose sole responsibility was to produce beer for the emperor. Pliny, in his Naturalis Historia, described and cataloged two major types of beer known in the empire: "zythum," of Egyptian origin, and "cerevisia," from Gaul and the Celtic regions. The renowned historian and naturalist wrote about the widespread presence of this beverage in the imperial provinces. In the capital of the Roman Empire, beer was recognized but not widely consumed; instead, it found use among women in cosmetics, such as cleaning the face or nourishing the skin.

With the increasing influx of Germanic tribes settling within the empire's boundaries before its fall, beer naturally became more widespread. These tribes brought their traditions with them, including the "gruit tax," a form of taxation based on the quantity of beer produced. During this period, beer was still crafted from fermented cereals but with the addition of various aromas, such as herbs, roots, and berries of all kinds. Some of these additives were dangerous, leading to hallucinogenic effects or even lethal poisoning.

This illustration, taken from the "Treatise of Medicine" by Hildebrand of Florence (1356), depicts the brewing process using barley and other grains. Within the brewery, you can see the vats where water and grains are combined, being continuously stirred by the master brewer.

THE ORIGINS OF BEER

As Christianity spread, monasteries soon became central points for rural populations regarding food supplies and the production of food and beverages, including beer. Monasteries, abbeys, and later castles played pivotal roles in the production of significant quantities of beer, significantly impacting everyday life. Unbeknownst to many, beer consumption helped people avoid diseases and poisoning common among those who consumed water, often contaminated and unhealthy.

Moreover, during periods of monastic fasting, beer was a permitted sustenance, considered "liquid bread." Consequently, the rules of various monastic orders allowed monks to consume substantial quantities of beer. The Venerable Bede even stipulated the precise amount of beer to be consumed at each meal. Participants at the council of Aquis Grana were allotted four liters each per day, in other cases five liters, and there are records of monasteries with limits of seven liters a day!

According to the strict rule of the order founded by the Irish Saint Columba, beer was substituted with water as a severe punishment. Among the legends surrounding Saint Columba, one narrates how he effortlessly burst a vat of beer that pagans were offering to Odin with a mere puff. He admonished them for wasting beer by giving it to the devil and encouraged them to obtain more, which he subsequently blessed before distributing. It emphasized that beer is a blessing from God but only if consumed in His name.

Queen of the Lombards Teodolinda, who established her court in Italy at Monza, was among the first to convert Germanic tribes to Catholicism. She maintained regular correspondence with Pope Gregory the Great and sent him a valuable gift: a large quantity of beer. Perhaps due to Rome's historical preference for wine, the Pope distributed it to the poor and pilgrims, reaffirming beer as "liquid bread" that nourished travelers.

The first monastic brewery mentioned in written records was the abbey of Weihehstephan, built in 724. In all monasteries, it was customary to categorize the wort based on quality. The "prima" or "melior" was reserved for consumption during Church-prescribed feast days, the "secunda" was for festive occasions and Sundays, while the "tertia" served as a daily sustenance, always regarded as "liquid bread." It was also offered to travelers and pilgrims who visited and stayed at the monasteries.

In monasteries, beer production began to be regulated and standardized in 1067 when Hildegard of Bingen, a botanist and abbess at the German monastery of Saint Rupert, experimented with hops as a flavoring agent. Historical documents indicate that hops, known to monastic herbalists for their calming and antibacterial properties, were first employed in beer production shortly after Charlemagne's coronation in 800. Initially used for its calming and disinfecting qualities during childbirth, Hildegard introduced hops instead of the herbs typically used in gruit. These herbs, due to their uncontrollable effects, including hallucinations and fatal poisoning, were now deemed perilous. Authorities even contemplated banning beer production due to these dangers. Some claimed that "witch hunts" were related to beer production, citing mysterious deaths of individuals who consumed beer prepared with unusual concoctions by women, leading to erratic and seemingly possessed behavior.

Gradually, beer production came under public control alongside home-made beer and that produced in monasteries and by the aristocracy in abbeys, monasteries, and castles. In the Anglo-Saxon world, this led to the establishment of public places where locals could trust the beer they consumed. These were known as "Public Houses," quickly abbreviated to "pub," a term still used worldwide to describe establishments where beer is served.

Unlike water, which often came from swamps or polluted wells, beer was considered a healthy beverage due to its production process. This belief is also reflected in the tales of Saint Arnold, now the patron saint of Belgian beer. It is said that in the 15th century, he saved the inhabitants of Soissons from a cholera epidemic by noting that those who drank beer were less susceptible to the disease than those who drank water. He invited the entire population to drink beer, which he stirred with his pastoral staff and blessed.

In any case, after Hildegard of Bingen's experiments, hop-based beer rapidly spread throughout Europe through trade and contacts with cities in the Hanseatic League. However, this shift didn't occur immediately in Great Britain, where local ales continued to be produced in public houses to the exclusion of continental hop-based beers. Beyond enhancing beer's flavor, hops' antiseptic properties also contributed to longer shelf life, ultimately allowing it to surpass other flavor enhancers.

The German Beer Purity Law, or Reinheitsgebot, was issued on April 13, 1516, by William IV of Bavaria. This law mandated that beer could only be crafted from water, barley malt, and hops. One may wonder about yeast's absence. At that time, the existence of the microorganism responsible for beer fermentation was unknown. Therefore, yeast was only included in the Purity Law during the industrial revolution.

Legend has it that this edict was initially intended to be in force for just one year, as a drastic solution to a severe famine. Aside from water and hops, brewers were allowed to use only barley malt to make beer to preserve other cereals, especially wheat, for solid food.

In reality, the Purity Law remained effective for a much longer period. In 1871, Bavaria agreed to become part of the German Empire under the condition that other states also adhered to it. More recently, the European Union requested the suspension of this law in Germany to facilitate the free circulation of beer produced in other states. Nonetheless, most brewers continue to adhere to its ingredient specifications, as wheat was subsequently accepted as an ingredient, and yeast was included once its discovery had occurred. This law also formerly regulated production and sale periods.

INDUSTRIAL BEER

Approximately a century after the enactment of the Purity Law, and after beer had made its way across the Atlantic Ocean to North America with the Pilgrim Fathers aboard the Mayflower, significant research and scientific discoveries occurred that would forever change beer production and consumption.

Antonie van Leeuwenhoek's experiments with his improved microscope led to the discovery of yeast's existence, identifying it as a crucial ingredient in beer production, even though it was not explicitly mentioned in the Purity Law. This discovery marked the emergence of three distinct beer production traditions in Europe: the German/Bohemian, Belgian, and Anglo-Saxon. However, this period was marked by considerable turbulence, including endless wars and severe economic crises that led to heavy taxation on beer.

In the Anglo-Saxon world, beer was still a part of workers' wages, provided at the end of a hard day's work. For instance, English porters received "porter" beer, which was produced by blending two different qualities and served in pint glasses filled to the brim. Foam was not viewed favorably in this context, as it would have reduced the quantity of beer received as payment.

In Belgium, the tradition of small brewers, starting with brewing monasteries, persisted, and the concept of local beer production remained deeply ingrained. In the German/Bohemian world, brewers began experimenting with large-scale beer production. Despite their differing approaches, all three traditions started to experiment with more innovative production systems before the French Revolution. They utilized new instruments made available by numerous scientific discoveries of the 18th century, such as the thermometer (invented by Fahrenheit in 1760) and the densitometer, introduced by Marin in 1770.

Another invention emerged that would transform not only beer-making but also the world itself. In 1765, James Watt invented the steam engine, paving the way for "steam-brewing," which expedited production and increased its scale.

Innovations continued to unfold. In the early 19th century, Daniel Wheeler developed a modern malt toaster, while in the later years of the century, Carl von Linde invented the refrigerator. This invention allowed beer to be produced year-round, eliminating the previous necessity of halting production in the spring and summer due to higher temperatures. Refrigeration improved product preservation and led to the development of the technique of "bottom fermentation" at temperatures below 53 °F (12 °C), involving a prolonged maturation period at a low temperature. Christian Hansen played a significant role in this technique by experimenting with yeast in the Carlsberg laboratories. He successfully isolated a single yeast cell and replicated it, gaining complete control over the most mysterious ingredient in beer-making. Brewers could now identify, isolate, and reproduce various types of yeast, using them specifically for different beers, while maintaining consistent flavors and characteristics.

Louis Pasteur further refined his pasteurization method to ensure the absence of infections or alterations in beer. This method extended the preservation period considerably, granting the product a longer shelf life, broader

This engraving from a book of the 17th century shows the hard work behind the
scenes in an old brewery, at a time when barrels were completely dominant.

THE ORIGINS OF BEER

Der Bier-Bräuer.
Scheitelt Wollust ein: so trinckt man Pein.

Der Durst nach Sachen dieser Zeit
erwartet bittre Süssigkeit:
Such, Seele, deinen Durst zu laben
im Brunnen der von Segen fleust,
und gegen Arme sich ergiest,
die in den Glauben Alles haben.

market access, and increased sales. Indicating the significance Pasteur attached to his beer experiments, one of his many books was titled "Studies on Fermentation," published in 1876.

The era of beer served in barrels, warm, flat, and dark-colored, produced on a small scale by numerous brewers scattered across the land using diverse yeasts, and served in wooden or earthenware containers, became a nostalgic relic of the past.

Industrial beer, on the other hand, was light in color, fresh, effervescent, served in elegant glasses, and produced on a larger scale by increasingly high-tech brewers. Beer was now distributed in barrels and glass bottles with hermetic seals, ensuring that the carbonation produced by the yeast remained intact until consumption, evident in its effervescence and foam. This marked the triumph of modern beer!

In the 20th century, the history of beer became intertwined with the complex history of the period, including revolutions, world wars, and prohibition. After the World Wars and subsequent reconstruction, the world was primed for mass production. Industrial beer in bottles, cans, and barrels became increasingly widespread, gradually overshadowing the thousands of smaller artisanal breweries that had emerged over the centuries. Large companies developed extensive distribution and marketing networks, turning beer into a global commodity.

THE RENAISSANCE OF BEER

The Western world experienced an economic boom in the 1960s and 1970s, accompanied by a sense of well-being after the dark periods of the two World Wars. This era witnessed remarkable changes in fashion, social interactions, leisure activities, and beer, too, played a role in these transformations. It was an age of music festivals, youth gatherings, and a newfound interest in local, high-quality products that told the stories of their places and the people behind them. Beer, once considered a "liquid food," had evolved into a beverage enjoyed purely for pleasure. It stood on the brink of another revolution, particularly in Britain and the United States.

In 1971, the Campaign for Real Ale (CAMRA) was founded in England, the same year the author was born. CAMRA remains an active association today, boasting over 150,000 members worldwide and organizing the renowned Great British Beer Festival (GBBF) annually—an event no beer enthusiast should miss. The term "Real Ale" was coined to distinguish traditional beers produced by small brewers using natural methods and processes from standard beers mass-produced by mega-corporations. Real Ales undergo secondary fermentation and are matured in barrels, from which they are served directly in pubs, typically utilizing methods like the "hand pump" or "pouring," which do not involve gas pressure to dispense the beer.

Thanks to CAMRA, there has been a resurgence of interest in rediscovering and appreciating traditional beer styles. These styles are slowly but steadily recapturing the hearts of a growing number of beer drinkers and enthusiasts.

In the United States, a network of small, local breweries began to sprout up everywhere, despite having nearly been wiped out by large-scale industrial production and the global dominance of light-colored lagers with nearly identical tastes and flavors. As often happens, this movement began with the passion of a diverse group of individuals.

One of these enthusiasts was entrepreneur Fritz Maytag, who purchased the Anchor Brewing Company in 1965. Maytag started producing "special" beers alongside the brewery's standard offerings, pioneering the concept of artisanal brewing and artisanal beer.

Subsequently, everyday people began to take an interest in home-brewing, reviving an ancient tradition, as mentioned earlier. Rather than being a mere trend or a reaction against mass production and rampant consumerism, home-brewing was born out of necessity. During that time, it was challenging to find more than a couple of high-quality beer varieties produced industrially in the United States. A visit to Belgium was enough to convince American beer enthusiasts that a change was overdue.

The next chapter was written by a passionate home-brewer who, in 1976, founded an artisanal brewery called The New Albion Brewery in Sonoma, California. Although it closed its doors a few years later, this endeavor inspired many others to follow suit, triggering a genuine renaissance in American brewing.

Thanks to individuals like Charlie Papazian (president of the American Brewers Association and founder of the American Home-Brewers Association) and small groups of enthusiasts, artisanal beer production became an expanding phenomenon. The number of small breweries in the USA began to grow, particularly between 1990 and 1995. In this period, the sector experienced a remarkable annual increase of 51%, following a 35% increase in 1990. This growth continues today, with over a thousand artisanal American brewers and brewpubs collectively producing several million barrels—a small yet significant portion of the total beer consumption in the United States.

This movement has also influenced Europe, where countries with a rich brewing tradition have revisited ancient practices, reintroduced forgotten production methods, flavors, and beer types, such as white beers and fruit-flavored beers, to name a few.

Today, the home-brewing movement and artisanal beer production have converted countries that were previously less interested in beer. For instance, Italy had only six artisanal producers in 1996, but it has now caught up with Belgium, boasting over 600 breweries.

The rapid expansion, while potentially leading to feelings of excess, confusion, and skepticism among the average beer drinker, may eventually face historical challenges, much like those experienced in the past. These challenges could pose more significant difficulties for small breweries than for large international conglomerates. However, as long as the philosophy underlying beer production remains rooted in joy, passion, quality, and professionalism, beer will remain secure and continue to evolve.

WHAT IS BEER?

I like to think of beer as a wonderful thing, good, upbeat, exhilarating, social, and wholesome. It's stunning in its wide range of colors, spanning from light yellow to the darkest black, touching every shade of amber, red, and brown. The foam too is a sight to behold, either bursting forth or reserved, varying in its persistence, but always telling a story! It might be a dense, creamy cap or a short-lived rise that pops up briefly for a swift nod before melding back into the beer.

Its countless bubbles are a joy, some tiny, others larger, some brilliantly white, some reminiscent of a cappuccino's hue.

Its scents and aromas are boundless, a reminder that it's born from nature's bounty and shaped by human hands: wildflowers, all sorts of fruits, aromatic herbs, spices, honey, and different smoked elements. And then, it can hit your palate as sweet, bitter, tangy, or even a touch salty, in various intensities and sequences.

It beckons us to observe it, to take in its fragrance, to savor its taste; and it also prompts us to lend an ear when we pop open a bottle and pour it out. Some beers glide out of the bottle as light as water, while others have the consistency of syrup. They want us to get to know them, to recognize their individuality, and to truly appreciate them.

You can enjoy it with close friends or fleeting acquaintances you might never cross paths with again. It's a treat for special occasions, celebrations, or just a daily drink with a meal, after a day's work, or in the evening. In tough times, beer provides an escape or a moment to reflect. However, beers are meant to be relished, to satisfy the senses, and to appreciate the mastery and dedication of the brewer behind it. There's joy in selecting the perfect glass for each beer from the myriad options: angular or smoothly contoured, stout or elongated, vintage or contemporary, ornate or simple. It's also fun to study the labels, appreciate the artwork, emblems, and details they provide, and not to forget, the elegance of the bottles and their seals. Even though its primary function is to be consumed, beer is sheer emotion! So, what exactly is beer? The question may sound straightforward, but it's not. First, as Lorenzo "Kuaska" Dabove, the Italian beer poet and my guide, once said, "there isn't just one beer; there are countless beers." We may have a notion of today's beers, but considering this beverage's age-old history and its independent evolution across various regions, it becomes evident how multifaceted it truly is, making it challenging to confine it to a single definition. Sure, beer is a drink. But originally, it was probably more akin to a watery grain-based soup. Yes, it's alcoholic due to fermentation, so moderation is essential. However, nowadays, we also have non-alcoholic beers, which despite their name, might contain trace amounts of alcohol, depending on each country's regulations. It's made from grains: barley, wheat, rye, sorghum, millet... Grains have always been humanity's primary food source because they're easily cultivated, have a long shelf life, and offer significant nutritional value from their starches (which translate to sugars). Yet, there are fermented drinks made from potatoes—a rich source of starch, but not a grain! It's flavored for sure. Over recent centuries, hops have been the dominant flavoring, but before that, an array of other additives was employed. It's primarily water-based. However, don't mistake water as merely a diluting agent. Unlike grapes which naturally contain a lot of water and yield a sugary liquid when crushed, grains lack water, producing only flour when "crushed." This makes water an indispensable ingredient in the brewing process. To provide a general description (with a more in-depth exploration later in this book), we can say beer results from the alcoholic fermentation by yeasts of a sugar-rich extract derived from malted barley and other grains, whether malted or not, and is flavored with hops.

THE RAW MATERIALS

WATER

Water is beer's primary ingredient, making it crucial. However, there isn't a one-size-fits-all water perfect for every beer variety. Instead, each beer demands a unique water type, characterized by a specific mineral salt concentration, hardness, and pH. These factors not only shape the beer's flavor but also impact various stages of its production. Moreover, water plays a vital role in cleaning and sanitizing equipment, leading to its substantial use in brewing. A contemporary challenge is to manage this water usage sustainably.

Historically, the presence of water with distinct characteristics in certain regions led to the birth of specific beer types exclusive to those locales. For instance, the Pils region in Bohemia, known for its soft water with minimal mineral salts, gave rise to the beers that still carry the "Pils" name today. In contrast, Ireland's hard water, abundant in mineral salts, is foundational to its iconic stouts. Nowadays, advances in water treatment technology enable brewers to tweak its composition based on specific production needs. This innovation means a particular beer type can maintain consistent qualities, irrespective of its production location.

YEAST (AND FERMENTATION)

"The brewer makes the wort, but it's the yeast that makes the beer." This adage, cherished by brewers, emphasizes that the true hero of beer-making is yeast, a microscopic single-celled organism that turns the wort crafted by the brewer into beer. Its scientific name, *Saccharomyces*, speaks volumes: it signifies a sugar (*-saccharo*) fungus (*-myces*).

Yeast cells metabolize sugars, yielding ethyl alcohol and carbon dioxide through the natural, albeit intricate, process known as alcoholic fermentation. A more colloquial, albeit less refined analogy, compares yeast metabolism to human digestion: we consume food and drink, and then eliminate waste. Similarly, during alcoholic fermentation, yeast consumes sugars and releases alcohol and carbon dioxide. The key distinction? Yeast's by-products are eagerly repurposed into our brews!

Thus, we're not discussing a process that merely "uses" alcohol (like some herbal liqueurs) or that "employs" carbon dioxide (as is the case with some carbonated beverages where it's added later). Instead, we're looking at a process that inherently "produces" both.

As yeast populates the wort, it continually reproduces (via cell division) until no sugars remain. Therefore, a beer's alcohol content hinges on the wort's sugar content. Given that this sugar originates from the cereal's starch, the more cereal used per volume of water, the stronger the resulting beer. In certain places, this principle is misinterpreted in legislation, which dubiously employs the term "double malt" to describe high-sugar, high-alcohol beers.

The abundant excess of yeast cells birthed during fermentation has been historically utilized in bread-making, coining the term "brewer's yeast."

Moreover, yeasts are instrumental in creating a spectrum of aromatic compounds, known as esters, which bestow upon beer its unique flavor profile and character.

There are numerous, carefully chosen yeast strains utilized in brewing. Generally, these yeasts fall into two major categories:

– *Saccharomyces cerevisiae:* Commonly known as "top-fermenting" yeasts. These yeasts operate at a warmer temperature, typically between 60 and 80 °F (15 and 25 °C). During fermentation, they tend to reside near the surface of the fermentation vessel, creating a dense layer of foam. Beers fermented with these yeasts are broadly categorized as "Ales."

– *Saccharomyces carlsbergensis:* These are "bottom-fermenting" yeasts. They function at cooler temperatures, usually below 53 °F (12 °C), and settle at the base of the fermentation vessel. These yeasts were first identified in the late 19th century within the labs of the renowned Danish Carlsberg brewery, which inspired their name. Historically, these yeasts were commonly found in the beers of northern Germany, where it was standard practice to age beer in cool cave environments. Beers produced with this yeast strain are termed "bottom-fermenting" and are generally referred to by the German term "Lager."

BARLEY MALT AND OTHER CEREALS

Next to water, barley malt is the primary ingredient in beer by volume. The process that turns barley into malt is known as "malting." In earlier times, malting was done within the brewery, marking the first step in the brewing process. Nowadays, this task has been handed off to specialized professionals called "maltsters" who operate outside the brewery. These maltsters are tasked with the crucial role of preparing a diverse "palette" of colors, tastes, and scents from which brewers can choose to craft their unique beer recipes. Malts not only dictate the beer's final color but also significantly influence its aroma and flavor profiles, often evoking notes of honey, caramel, biscuit, and coffee.

So, what exactly is malting? To start, barley grains are soaked in water. This initiates their germination process. During this phase, enzymes inside the grains activate, working to convert the seed's stored reserves to nourish the emerging sprout. These invaluable enzymes become crucial partners for brewers when preparing the wort. Following this, the germinated grains are dried, promptly halting the growth of the germ and its tiny roots. Depending on how far the grain has grown and the specifics of the drying process—both duration and

temperature—the resulting malt can vary significantly in chemical composition. By adjusting these factors, maltsters can produce malts with distinct colors, flavors, and aromas, all of which contribute to a wide variety of beers.

While crafting a particular beer, brewers primarily utilize four foundational malt types, each abundant in enzymes: Pils and Pale (on the lighter end of the spectrum), and Vienna and Munich (with a reddish-brown hue). To these bases, they might add special malts—those that have been caramelized or toasted—but these are generally in smaller proportions.

Barley malt's reputation is so ingrained in the brewing world that, even though other grains like wheat, oats, rye, and spelt can also be malted, the term "malt" typically refers to barley malt. Tradition dictates the use of specific grains for certain beers. For instance, Weiss beers use malted wheat, Blanches favor unmalted wheat, while Roggenbier and the contemporary Rye IPA lean on malted rye.

HOPS

Though hops (*Humulus lupulus*) were introduced into beer-making during the Middle Ages, today they reign supreme in the brewing process. Hops are best known for imparting that distinctive bitter taste to beer. Moreover, their aroma can vary considerably based on where they're grown. Their natural antiseptic and antioxidant properties also make them a practical addition, acting as preservatives. This was a vital attribute in the 18th century when India Pale Ales (IPAs) brewed in England had to survive the long voyage to India, and they did so while retaining their distinct flavors, thanks largely to the generous hop content.

The hop plant is a perennial climber, related to hemp. It thrives in cold to temperate climates, specifically between latitudes 35° and 55° in both the Northern and Southern Hemispheres. The plant produces both male and female flowers, but only the female ones, rich in lupulin, essential oils, and resins, are harnessed for brewing. Numerous hop varieties exist, each with unique characteristics— much like the grapes used in winemaking. These hops can range in aroma from herbaceous, spicy, floral, and resinous to fruity and balsamic. Additionally, some hops are distinctly bitter, while newer hop breeds have successfully married bitterness with aromatic qualities.

In the ever-evolving world of beer, it's not uncommon to find unique ingredients like honey, ginger, coffee, fruits (like cherries, strawberries, raspberries, figs, and chestnuts), spices (from a wide array to star anise and cinnamon), and even roots such as licorice and gentian. While some ingredients have deep-rooted traditions, others represent modern brewers' penchant for experimentation. These innovative brewmasters relish in pushing boundaries, creating exciting, and sometimes even audacious, flavor combinations.

HOW BEER IS MADE

Brewing is an art as ancient as humanity, both simple and complex. It's clear there's no one-size-fits-all way to brew beer. In this section, we'll explore the main steps in the beer-making process, with later chapters diving into the specific production techniques for different beer styles.

Returning to the idea that yeast is the star of beer-making, it's clear that every step is designed to cater to this microorganism. It ensures that it can effectively "eat" the simple sugars and "produce" ethyl alcohol, carbon dioxide, and an array of compounds that give beer its unique aromas and flavors.

The first task for a brewer is to nail down the kind of beer they want to produce. This includes its color, alcohol content, aroma, taste, and overall balance. Once they've settled on a vision, they create a recipe, selecting from a range of ingredients to get the desired outcome.

After finalizing the recipe, the brewer can begin the actual brewing process. This is split into two main phases: the hot side, which encompasses mashing, wort separation, grain sparging, boiling, the whirlpool process, and cooling and oxygenation. Following that is the cold side, which can be divided into primary fermentation, secondary fermentation, and maturation.

THE HOT SIDE

The hot side operates at elevated temperatures and, in brewing lingo, it's referred to as "the brew." This step unfolds in a brewhouse, which houses a setup of large containers. These containers often come with built-in mixers, pipes, pumps, and temperature gauges. Many of us imagine these containers as the shiny copper vats prominently showcased in numerous breweries. However, these days, the use of copper has been phased out in favor of stainless steel. This shift is because stainless steel is both safer for brewing and more convenient to use. Nowadays, copper is mainly reserved for the aesthetic appeal, serving as a decorative outer shell for these vessels.

MASHING

The goal of this stage is to produce sweet wort by converting starch into sugars. In the mash tun, the right mix of water and grains come together, forming a sort of mushy concoction. While the water may undergo varying levels of treatment, it's essential that it's warm — not cold or boiling — to allow the enzymes, which were activated during the malting process, to break down the starch. All grains, whether malted or not, are coarsely ground with a two-fold objective: to break apart the grain while preserving the outer shell (the glume) as much as possible. This method ensures the grainy part interacts with the hot water, facilitating enzyme activity present in the malted grain. The husks, meanwhile, play a critical role in the ensuing filtration step.

Various enzymes exist in the malt, each with a unique function and specific operational temperature. By adjusting the temperature, the brewer can control the activity of these enzymes to achieve the desired beer attributes outlined in the recipe.

The pivotal enzymes are those that handle saccharification: Alpha-amylase and Beta-amylase. These enzymes efficiently break down the starch molecule, which is made up of lengthy chains of complex sugars, converting it into simpler sugar molecules. Beta-amylase primarily produces maltose, a disaccharide consisting of two fully fermentable glucose molecules. These can be wholly consumed by the yeasts, resulting in the production of alcohol and carbon dioxide. On the other hand, Alpha-amylase creates maltodextrin. These are polysaccharides with 3 to 17 glucose units connected, and since yeasts can't metabolize them, they remain in the final beer, imparting body and a hint of sweetness.

Other enzymes, like proteolytic enzymes, are tasked with breaking down proteins that might cloud the finished beer.

Once the starch has been fully converted into sugars, which typically takes around an hour and a half, the temperature is raised to halt enzyme activity. This also makes the mix more liquid, prepping it for the next step: filtration.

FILTRATION

The goal of this stage is to extract the sweet liquid, separating it from the solid remnants of the crushed grains. The concoction is moved to another vessel called a lautering tun where the wort is introduced. This tun has a slotted false bottom that allows the heavier solids to settle. This results in a "lautering bed", a thick, layered mesh of husks, grain fragments, and flour that serves as a natural filter. This bed permits the sweet liquid to seep through while capturing even the smallest particulate matter. If the grains, especially the husks, are milled too finely, this step would be compromised, jeopardizing the entire brewing process. Simultaneously, the sweet wort is gradually gathered in a separate vessel where it will be boiled.

RINSING

The filtration bed is then rinsed with fresh hot water to extract any sugars that might still be trapped in the grain bed and to achieve the desired volume of wort. It's important to remember that during the upcoming boiling phase, a significant portion of the wort will evaporate. To account for this loss, brewers make volume adjustments during this rinsing, or "sparging," stage. Typically, this process of filtration, sparging, and transferring the wort to the boiling kettle takes about an hour and a half. The leftover grain from this step is often repurposed as livestock feed, especially for cattle and pigs.

BOILING AND THE WHIRLPOOL

It's during this step that hops make their entrance. The wort's temperature is raised to 210 °F and it's boiled for up to two hours to ensure sterilization. Additionally, at this temperature, the resins from the hops undergo isomerization, dissolving and releasing their bitterness. This boiling stage also prompts proteins to coagulate, leading to clearer finished beer. Undesirable aromatic components, like DMS (dimethyl sulfide), are driven

off during boiling. However, this boiling can also risk the loss of some desirable hop aromas, so aromatic hops are often added during the last minutes of boiling or even afterward. For beers with a pronounced hop character, post-boil, the wort might pass through containers packed with hops to maximize aroma extraction. Alternatively, brewers might employ dry-hopping, adding aromatic hops directly to the fermenter. At these cooler temperatures, a different bouquet of aromas and flavors emerges.

By the end of this stage, the wort has accumulated residues from hopping and protein formation. Before moving it to the fermentation tank, where the eager yeasts will take over, it needs to be cleared of solid particles. To do this, the wort is swirled, creating a vortex. Centripetal force gathers all the solids in the center of the vessel. Using an opening on the outer edge, the brewer then drains the clarified wort into the fermentation tank.

A few crucial steps remain. The boiling wort needs to be cooled to a temperature suitable for the yeast; otherwise, the yeast could perish. This cooling must be swift to avoid contamination from bacteria and wild yeasts, which thrive in this sterile, sugary environment. Typically, a plate heat exchanger or a "tube in tube" system is used for cooling. During this cooling process, the wort is also oxygenated, supplying the yeast with the oxygen required for reproduction. After a long day, the "brew" process concludes.

FERMENTATION

The yeast, once adequately prepped, is introduced into the wort at the optimal temperature and gets to work. It has a wealth of simple sugars to convert into ethyl alcohol and carbon dioxide. But smartly, before diving into this primary task, it first consumes all the available oxygen. This helps the yeast multiply, producing new offspring that will assist in this extensive process. After this seemingly quiet phase (known as latency), the real alcoholic fermentation kicks off.

PRIMARY FERMENTATION

Yeast operates like a mini chemical powerhouse, methodical, highly efficient, and unrelenting, working around the clock as long as it has sustenance. Early on, when it has access to a plethora of simple sugars, its activity is so intense that it can cause a spike in the fermenter's temperature. That's why there's a need to monitor and control it with a cooling system to prevent overheating. Left unchecked, a dangerous cycle could ensue: the temperature goes up, accelerating the yeast's activity, which in turn generates even more heat. In such stressful thermal conditions, yeast can produce undesirable aromas and flavors that could spoil the beer. Push the temperature too high, and the yeast might even die, halting fermentation entirely.

However, when kept at the ideal temperature, yeast can work wonders, efficiently converting simpler sugars like glucose and maltose over roughly a week, while imparting its unique aromatic and taste profile. Once this phase concludes, primary fermentation is done.

HOW BEER IS MADE

SECONDARY FERMENTATION

During this stage, the pace of fermentation slows down substantially, and the beer's temperature drops. A significant number of yeast cells become dormant and gradually settle to the bottom. As they descend, they pull down many other particles, particularly protein compounds, initiating the beer's clarification process, which will only conclude in the subsequent maturation stage.

Yet, the beer still contains numerous active yeast cells and remnants of simple sugars. Among these are maltodextrin molecules. All of these will persist in the final beer, with the exception of maltotriose—a basic compound made up of three individual glucose molecules. This sugar can be slowly processed by yeast (though not all strains) during secondary fermentation. The duration of this secondary fermentation can vary greatly depending on the beer type. For more straightforward brews, this phase might be skipped entirely. But for more intricate beers, like English Barley Wines or the German Doppel Bock, it can be quite time-intensive.

MATURATION

After fermentation concludes, the beer needs to be cooled to a brisk 32°F (0°C). This cold temperature promotes the natural settling of the yeast and aids in refining the beer's taste and stabilizing its attributes. While you can rapidly and more aggressively remove the yeast through filtration, centrifugation, or by adding colloidal substances, these methods don't hasten maturation. Unique brews, such as Lambic or other barrel-aged beers, may even require years of maturation.

Once the maturation phase is over, the beer is primed for bottling or canning. Depending on the brewer's preferences and the beer style, you can bottle beers that are already carbonated or induce carbonation through secondary fermentation inside the bottle. For the latter, the beer is bottled or canned "flat", with a small amount of sugar (and sometimes yeast) added. This minor addition sparks a modest secondary fermentation. As these containers are sealed tight, the generated carbon dioxide remains dissolved in the beer, bestowing it with its signature fizz and froth.

When it comes to packaging, large-scale brewers often opt to pasteurize their finished beer to ensure longer shelf-life and stability. This process ensures any lingering bacteria are exterminated. However, it also terminates any remaining yeast. While this method guarantees a stable product, aficionados with a keen palate and nose might find the taste a tad underwhelming.

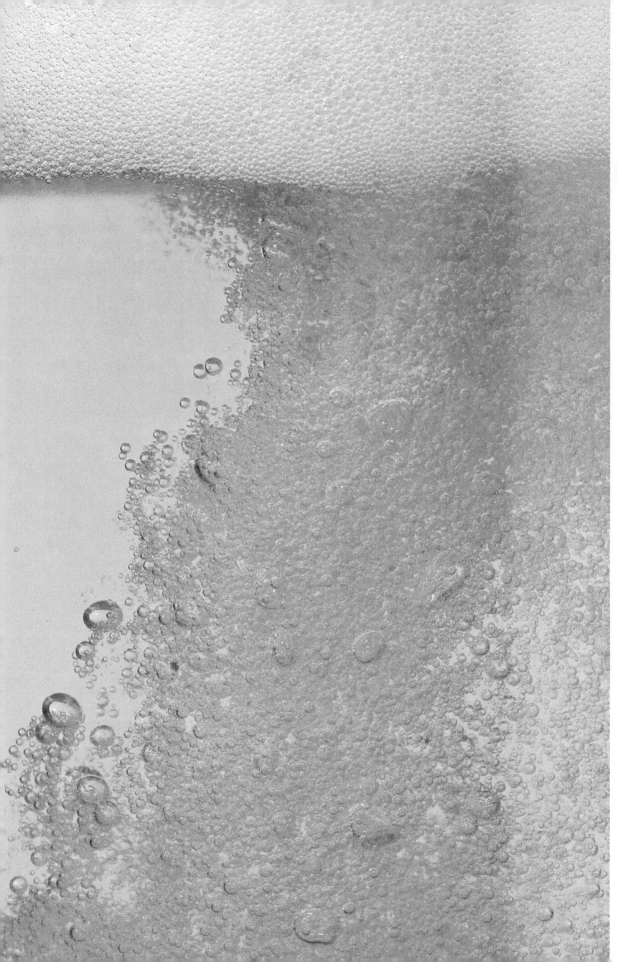

SPONTANEOUS FERMENTATION

Beer is a discovery believed to be entirely fortuitous, tracing back to the dawn of civilization when humans settled and began cultivating cereals. The earliest known mention of beer dates back to 3800 B.C. on a tablet that contains a hymn to Sikuru (thought to mean "liquid bread" in Sumerian), discovered in Nineveh, present-day Iraq. Those early beers were produced without sophisticated instruments, in less-than-hygienic conditions, and, most notably, without any knowledge of yeast.

However, it's essential not to dismiss this early history entirely. Beer production evolved over the years, involving the malting of cereal grains and the introduction of new techniques. While the lack of knowledge about yeast was a secondary issue, the brewing world gradually divided into two groups. Some brewers collected what they sensed was the key ingredient responsible for wort fermentation, transferring it from one vat to another to consistently produce the same beer. Others relied entirely on nature, allowing the wort to transform into beer "miraculously" without intervention, resulting in longer production times and no control over the process.

The latter approach was particularly captivating: spontaneous fermentation. It resisted numerous challenges, much like the Gallic village of Asterix. Despite facing hardships and legal ambiguities, it survived, primarily in a small region between Brussels and Pajottenland, southwest of Brussels along the River Senne. While there were once many brewers in and around Brussels producing Lambic beer (beer with spontaneous fermentation), only a handful remain today. Within Brussels itself, only one has persisted—Cantillon. The brewery is still owned and managed by the same family, with Jean Van Roy, the great-grandson of the founder Paul Cantillon, overseeing Lambic production and decision-making. The brewery has also transformed into a museum dedicated to Lambic beer.

A visit to the Gueuze Museum (Rue Gheude 56, Anderlecht, Brussels), where you can explore maturation cellars filled with barrels, view copper brewing kettles, and inspect 19th-century equipment, will provide a better understanding of this fascinating world than any words can convey.

Spontaneous fermentation in beer embodies biodiversity, as the wort ferments thanks to naturally occurring yeasts and bacteria present in the air. Their concentrations vary from brewery to brewery and from region to region. Today, we can isolate, count, and classify these yeasts and bacteria into groups and subgroups, but variations occur from year to year. These differences manifest in the unique flavors and characteristics of beers, closely tied to the cellars where they are crafted and influenced by the local flora.

Brewers have limited control over this process. At most, they can influence the wort production, using unmalted wheat to aid wild yeast in the fermentation process. They may also manipulate barrels to impart

additional character. However, the primary factor is waiting for nature to take its course. Apart from industrial methods that tend to homogenize the results, these beers are exclusively brewed during the cold season, from the first frost to early spring. This prevents undesirable bacteria from overpowering the favored house guest—*Brettanomyces* yeast, the star of these beers. *Brettanomyces*, along with its many brethren (various wild yeast strains), lactic bacteria, acetobacteria, and others, each play their unique roles, making significant contributions, whether large or small.

For instance, Cantillon, one of the notable breweries, has had over 100 different yeast types identified by research scientists at the University of Louvain, including various *Saccharomyces* and *Brettanomyces* strains, alongside 27 acetobacteria types and 38 lactic bacteria strains—all contributing to the wort fermentation. While this information dates back a few years, it's likely that new actors of lesser importance have since emerged.

However, spontaneous fermentation isn't unique to Pajottenland. In Flanders, close by, you'll find the Reds of Flanders, a blend of top-fermented beer with fermentation involving lactic and acetic bacteria in large oak vats. Here, the acetic notes dominate the aroma, softened by sweetness. In the same region, Oud Bruin (Old Brown) beers feature added lactic bacteria alongside top-fermenting yeasts, imparting depth and broadening the flavor spectrum.

Belgium serves as the guardian of these traditions, but their survival is also due to foreign markets. Countries like the United States, Scandinavia, and Italy have played a significant role. Moreover, an increasing number of brewers in these countries are focusing on extended barrel aging, both new and used, to achieve aromatic profiles reminiscent of spontaneous fermentations. In essence, very few brewers are genuinely attempting completely spontaneous, or nearly spontaneous, fermentation today.

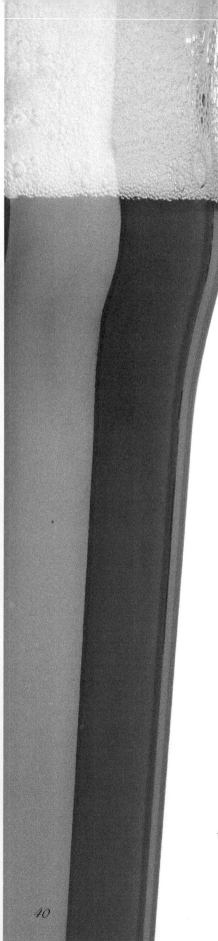

TOP FERMENTATION

"Top fermentation" refers to the process of brewing beers where yeast ferments in the upper part of the fermentation vat, typically at higher temperatures than those used for bottom fermentation, around 70 °F (20-22 °C). Nevertheless, as we will see, there are exceptions.

These beers are commonly referred to as Ales, indicating the type of fermentation, much like Lagers are associated with bottom fermentation. However, this term, while useful for identifying the yeast type used, encompasses a vast family of beers with significant differences among them.

Top fermentation is characteristic of Great Britain and Belgium, playing a significant role in the renaissance of beer in the United States and subsequently around the world. It has effectively drawn a line between "supermarket" beers, mostly utilizing bottom-fermenting yeast and often considered "flat" in terms of flavors and character, and craft beers produced by independent micro-breweries. The latter often offer an explosion of unique flavors and personality. Nevertheless, not all bottom-fermented beers taste the same, and some of them are genuine masterpieces. Similarly, a small producer can create exceptional beers using either top fermentation or bottom fermentation.

Before the isolation of yeast strains and their commercial availability, beers were fermented by a mixture of natural yeasts that had essentially self-selected over centuries, adapting to specific environmental conditions (temperature and alcohol content) with the fittest yeast strains surviving. These yeasts thrived within the same beers, proliferated, and were reused in a continuous chain from one batch to another, akin to the concept of a "mother dough" in baking. These yeast strains, passed down through generations, now belong to the *Saccharomyces cerevisiae* lineage, which has given rise to more modern yeast strains. These are known as top-fermenting yeasts.

Britain was the pioneer in turning brewing into an industrial process, replacing the alchemical laboratory or farm-like environment that was the norm previously. In more recent times, Real Ales have experienced a

HOW BEER IS MADE

resurgence, thanks to the efforts of volunteers in the 1970s, and they continue to thrive. Styles like Bitter, Porter, Stout, and India Pale Ale originated in Britain and subsequently spread to Ireland, Russia (Imperial Russian Stout), and even found new life in the United States. Top fermentation proved to be a perfect match for English barley (and malt) and English hops. Over time, the earthy hop flavors and biscuity malts harmonized with the yeasts, which remained somewhat hidden in taste, except for the occasional hints of sulfur and diacetyl (buttery notes) as the beer matured. These yeasts also worked well with cask conditioning, allowing Anglo-Saxon breweries to produce beer more quickly since there was a relatively short time between brewing and serving. It also gave rise to professional publicans who took care of the beer directly in their cellars.

Belgium stands out as the country where top-fermenting yeasts have demonstrated their full potential, not merely as fermentation agents but as essential contributors to beer flavor. In British beers, yeast typically plays a background role, responsible for alcohol content, while in Belgium, it often plays a primary role in shaping the beer's taste.

To some extent, this reflects the Belgian brewing world's approach: when nature doesn't dictate the beer's character (as in spontaneous fermentation), yeast is selected to do so directly. While Britain has primarily focused on barley cultivation, malting techniques, and hop studies, Belgium has emphasized yeast research, to the extent of almost overlooking hop plantations (though they have seen a recent resurgence).

Over the years, Belgian brewers have selected unique yeast strains that give their beers a signature flavor unique to the brewery where it's produced. Producers without access to a laboratory and their yeast strains struggle to recreate the same flavor profiles when they switch to a new batch of *Saccharomyces* from a general supplier. Some breweries possess yeast strains that can function at different temperatures, creating beers with varying flavor profiles.

Some Belgian beers are, quite literally, yeast masterpieces. They boast high alcohol levels and attenuation, resulting in delightful dryness, as well as esters that significantly contribute to aroma and flavor. For example, the spicy, almost smoky notes of Saison beers, the fruity characteristics of Dubbel, Quadrupel, and similar styles, and the phenolic notes of Tripel all owe their sensations to the right yeast strains.

The Orval Trappist brewery, for instance, maintains a microbiology laboratory that monitors the yeast strain isolated years ago. They also offer the yeast to other brewers upon request, provided they collect it in person. This yeast is unique and used exclusively for the beer brewed in the monastery, making it unmistakable.

Even in Germany, top-fermenting yeasts find use, especially in wheat beers. In a Weizen (or Weissbier) beer of this style, yeast plays a prominent role in shaping taste. The sensation of ripe banana, for example, results from a chemical compound (isoamyl acetate) produced by the yeast during fermentation, along with phenolic compounds that contribute clove-like flavors. While hops are present, they don't dominate, and the grist provides a mouthfeel with the astringency characteristic of wheat.

BOTTOM FERMENTATION

Bottom-fermented beers earned their name because they're brewed using yeasts that ferment at the bottom of fermentation tanks. These beers are popularly known as "Lagers," derived from the German word for storage or warehouse.

Interestingly, the term "Lager" doesn't define specific styles or flavors. Much like how "Ale" refers to top-fermented beers, "Lager" is broad in its classification. The word harkens back to the early days when beers were aged for weeks in cellars or tunnels beneath breweries to escape the heat. Before the advent of gas refrigeration, the only method to keep beer cool was storing barrels in these cellars, where temperatures remained stable. Often, these tunnels were packed with ice sourced from nearby lakes or rivers by the end of winter, ensuring that the beers were kept close to 32 °F (0 °C)—the optimal maturation temperature.

Two significant figures played roles in the evolution of bottom-fermented beers: the German Gabriel Sedlmayr and the Dane Emil Christian Hansen. Sedlmayr adopted British mechanized beer production techniques from the 1830s and introduced them to Germany, notably scaling up Munich's historic Spaten brewery. He made vital changes in the malting process and integrated British production techniques, such as using the saccharometer, to maximize ingredient and equipment utilization.

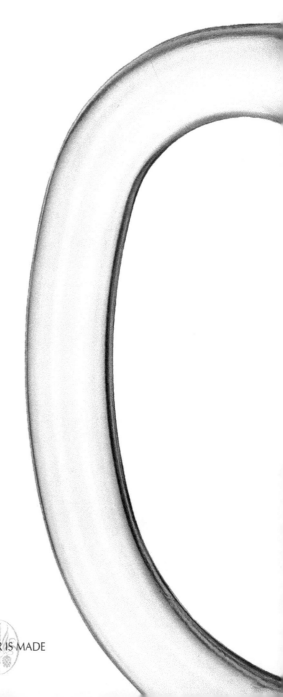

HOW BEER IS MADE

Hansen, a mycologist employed by Carlsberg in Copenhagen from 1870 until his death in 1909, played a pivotal role in the development of modern lagers. Through his research, Hansen was the first to successfully isolate a pure yeast cell responsible for the fermentation of wort. This yeast strain was subsequently named *Saccharomyces carlsbergensis* after the brewery where it was isolated. Hansen's work also demonstrated the possibility of reproducing this yeast strain in a laboratory setting.

The combined contributions of Gabriel Sedlmayr's industrial brewing methods from Britain and Emil Christian Hansen's yeast isolation research paved the way for the world of modern lagers. These lagers, most of which are prominently displayed in colored bottles with vibrant labels on supermarket shelves worldwide, have become a global phenomenon.

Bottom fermentation isn't limited to beers produced by rapid industrial processes with a focus on marketing over ingredients. It is also a preferred method for crafting complex beers, which necessitate extended aging at very low temperatures, sometimes lasting two or three months, to achieve the perfect balance and a clean, fragrant aroma. The yeast strains used in bottom fermentation contribute minimally to flavor or aroma due to the low temperatures at which they work. Fermentation typically starts below 60 °F (15 °C), with maturation occurring at around 32 °F (0 °C). This allows the flavor of hops from regions like Hallertau, Tettnang, and other parts of Germany and Bohemia to take center stage, rather than the malt. The prolonged cellar or refrigerated aging process enables yeast to slowly absorb any off-flavors as they develop. These off-flavors can include diacetyl, which imparts an unpleasant sensation of fruity butter, and various sulfur compounds that produce effects ranging from the classic smell of rotten eggs to notes of cooked vegetables. Once the yeast has absorbed these off-flavors, it settles at the bottom, resulting in a visually clear and appealing beer.

Many of the best session beers, known for being easy to drink, slightly bitter, and low in alcohol, belong to this category. Examples include Pils, Hell, and many others. In Franconia, every brewery produces its own interpretations of traditional lagers, including Ungespundet, Keller, Zwickl, Landbier, Pils, Lager, Export Lager, Bock, Doppelbock, Schwartz, among many others. These beers, all starting from a shared idea, exhibit incredible diversity due to each brewery's unique approach. Despite the constraints of the German Beer Purity Law, which has guided beer production for centuries and allows brewers significant freedom, it does not guarantee the quality of the beers, which can vary from excellent to poor, even when adhering to its provisions.

The world of bottom fermentation remains closely linked to the cities where individual beers originate. This is primarily due to the influence of local water characteristics, which result in different types of barley malts and, in turn, individual styles like Münchner, Dortmunder, Pils, Vienna Lagers, and more.

Maintaining stringent hygiene in a brewery that employs bottom-fermenting yeast is crucial, akin to an operating theater's cleanliness. This applies whether the fermentation tank is open to the air without a cover or not. Modern brewers, clad in pristine white coats, walk on polished floors and oversee gleaming steel equipment. This stark contrast is a far cry from the past when beers were matured in wooden barrels, inheriting various aromas and flavors in the process.

Industrial lagers have become ubiquitous worldwide, but bottom-fermented production has thrived in response. In the United States, for instance, two new beer styles—American Pilsner Lager and Amber Lager—have been introduced. These styles are characterized by generous additions of American hops, pushing the limits of bitterness and aromas beyond the original German lagers.

Italy has also embraced bottom-fermented beers, with wonderful examples that blend traditional styles with Italian innovation. The northeastern part of Italy, influenced by the Austrian brewing tradition during the Austro-Hungarian Empire, has maintained a strong presence of bottom fermentation. While bottom-fermented craft beers are a minority in Italy, they are often both interesting and well-crafted. Consequently, the Italian national competition "Beer of the Year," organized by Unionbirrai, now includes an Italian Lager category for clear, low-alcohol Italian beers inspired by the German brewing world.

Throughout its history, the Netherlands has drawn inspiration from both southern and western brewing traditions. While some Dutch breweries have embraced the German style, recently, some Dutch brewers have rekindled their country's ancient brewing traditions. However, many regions of the Netherlands have predominantly embraced industrial beer production without significant experimentation or research.

SERVING BEER

While many of us might think there's a strict art to beer serving, here's a simple golden rule: do it your way! You won't meet any dire fate from a less-than-perfectly served beer or one chugged straight from an ice-cold bottle. However, if you're aiming to get the most out of your beer experience, take a deep breath and remember: there's no singular "right" way to serve beer. There are just a few guidelines to consider, and the rest is up to you!

- First and foremost, it's undeniable that serving beer is both a delicate and critical step in ensuring the best drinking experience—or if done incorrectly, potentially diminishing its quality.
- Secondly, there are several key factors that play pivotal roles in this process, all equally significant: the beer's temperature, the chosen glass and its preparation, the method of dispensing (or the technique when pouring from the bottle), and of course, the specific type of beer you're serving.

We can categorize the primary methods of serving beer into two main approaches: dispensing from kegs and pouring from bottles. It's the seasoned bartender's call to choose whether to serve the beer via a pressurized tap, a manual hand pump, or simply by gravity (that is, pouring directly from the cask).

DRAUGHT BEER

raft dispensing is by far the most popular method of erving beer. It utilizes gas, which is forcibly injected o create pressure within the airtight keg, pushing the eer through a chilled line and out through the tap andle. Naturally, only food-grade certified gases are sed, like carbon dioxide or a blend of carbon dioxide nd nitrogen. This system is adaptable for most beer yles worldwide. However, if rushed, the beer can ome out too cold and overly carbonated. But with a eticulous and professional approach, adjusting the ngle and distance of the glass, it's entirely possible to erve outstanding beers with the perfect carbonation vel, topped with a beautiful foam head, at just the ght temperature.

THE HAND PUMP

The hand pump, also known as a "beer engine," is a classic method of serving beer. With its distinct long handle and iconic swan-necked nozzle, it allows for beer to be served even if the keg is at a distance, commonly stored in a cooler cellar or a fridge right below the bar. The mechanism is straightforward: manually pulling the handle creates a vacuum, drawing the beer up from the cask. Occasionally, a "sparkler" is affixed to the nozzle's end. This device, equipped with multiple tiny holes, makes the beer flow more turbulently and under higher pressure, generating a plethora of micro-bubbles. The result? A smooth, dense, creamy head. Beers served this way tend to be less carbonated, preventing a bloated feeling and are best enjoyed slightly chilled. This dispensing method is often favored for many top-fermented beers in both British and American styles, and offers swift service.

FROM THE CASK BY GRAVITY

This method is the oldest and most straightforward way to serve beer. Simply insert a tap into the barrel, and due to gravity, the beer naturally flows out. However, as the beer exits, air replaces it, which can cause oxidation. Hence, it's crucial to empty the barrel promptly, especially if it's not chilled. Today, this traditional method is mostly employed in the UK for serving Real Ale. But you might also find it in places like Bamberg, Germany, known for its Rauchbier, or in Prague, the birthplace of the Pils. If you ever witness the ritual of opening a cask, perhaps covered in unique cooling jackets, don't be taken aback if someone comes forward with a hammer. They're just fitting the tap! However, if they're shaky and miss their mark, those nearby might get an unexpected beer shower. Generally, don't anticipate beers served like this to be very foamy or fizzy.

The three serving techniques described should not be viewed as inherently "right" or "wrong." Factors like the amount of foam, temperature, and serving time are not absolute, and personal preferences play a significant role. Just as you wouldn't wear heavy mountain boots for an athletics competition or use a Ferrari for a cross-country outing, it's important to consider the appropriate context for each serving method. Everyone is entitled to their choices, but it's essential not to be surprised if the outcome doesn't align with expectations.

For example, when beer is served with a hand pump, one should not expect a sparkling, ice-cold beverage. Conversely, when served with a pressure pump and the glass tilted close to the nozzle, you can anticipate a beautiful, substantial head of foam, which might lead to a bloated sensation. Understanding the diverse styles and customs of various countries is crucial. In Belgium, a notably impressive head of foam is customary, and it's common to "cut it" level with the rim of the glass using a small utensil like a spatula. In Germany, the foam may appear creamy and overflow the glass's edge. In contrast, in England, you might not find any foam at all. None of these practices are inherently wrong; each reflects regional styles and traditions.

Using the correct glass for each type of beer is of utmost importance. Nowadays, specific styles of beer are associated with particular types of glasses, which can be somewhat confusing. Ensuring that the glass is perfectly clean is crucial, but it should not have any traces of detergent or rinse aid, as these can hinder the formation of a lively foam. Additionally, it's essential to rinse the inside of the glass generously with the coldest water possible to prevent subjecting the beer to a thermal shock.

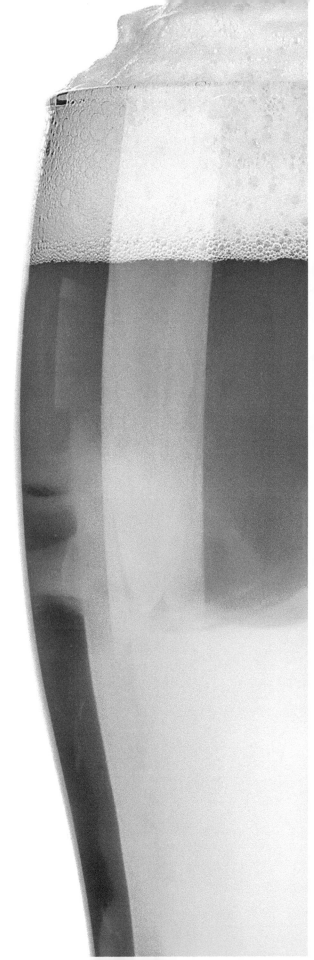

BOTTLED BEER

When dealing with bottled beer, one of the most critical considerations—prior to discussing the beer's service—is the proper storage, especially when the beer is neither pasteurized nor re-fermented in the bottle. There's a generally accepted rule: bottles should be stored vertically, unless they are sealed with a cork, and kept in a dark, cool place. The duration for which bottled beer can be stored varies depending on the type. Some beers, like APA or Hell, are best consumed when young, while others, such as strong Barley Wine, benefit from extended aging, continuing to develop and improve gracefully.

When serving beer from a bottle, equal care should be taken in selecting the appropriate glass. Choose a glass that suits the beer style, ensure it's thoroughly washed, and dried properly.

While today, we naturally think of using glasses made of glass for serving beer, this was a luxury available only to a select few in the past. Most people drank their beer from jugs made of wood, clay, or metal. Some even used leather vessels coated with tar. The traditional lidded tankards, which may appear quaint today, served practical purposes, especially in rural settings or for outdoor beer consumption. The lid helped keep insects and midges out of the tankard. Although some claim it also prevented oxidation, it's a minor consideration in comparison.

Another critical aspect to consider when serving beer is the temperature. Serving temperature can vary widely, ranging from 40°F (5°C) to 65°F (18°C), or even higher for specialty beers like Gluhbier, a spicy winter beer served hot, similar to mulled wine. Nowadays, beer labels and brewery websites increasingly provide guidance on the ideal serving temperature, which is an excellent starting point. In general, simpler beers like light Lagers are best enjoyed when served quite cold, while more complex varieties like Belgian Dubbels and English Old Ales should be served slightly warmer, typically above 50-53°F (10-12°C). This is based on the principle that excessively low temperatures can impair the beer's flavors.

It's crucial to allow the beer to exude its aromas, and excessive cold can hinder this. Extremely cold temperatures also affect taste perception, essentially numbing the taste buds.

Consider that the "serving temperature" should match the beer's temperature in the glass. Achieving this requires factoring in the ambient temperature, particularly on hot summer days, as well as the time needed to serve the beer.

At this point, you have bottles of beer that have been expertly brewed by the brewer, stored correctly, and prepared at the right temperature, along with clean and suitable glasses.

Now, let's open the bottle. This routine operation can be a pleasurable experience and provide additional insights. Develop the habit of listening for the hissing sound as the pressure escapes, observe the dense gas forming in the bottle neck, and watch as it escapes slowly and cautiously. Pay attention to the bubbles rising to the surface, whether they are large or small. If necessary, tilt the bottle slightly to provide more space for them.

Finally, it's time to pour the beer. Position the bottle's mouth close to the glass, leaving an inch or two of space between them. Tilt the glass at an angle of about 45° and start pouring so that the beer slides along the side of the glass. Do this neither too roughly nor too slowly. Once the bottom of the glass is covered with both beer and foam, straighten the glass and continue pouring steadily and without hesitation into the center of the glass until it's full. Don't worry about creating a substantial head of foam, as this is desirable and can occupy up to 75% of the glass's volume.

If necessary, adjust the distance between the glass and the bottle to control the foam level. Avoid overzealous actions like raising the bottle several feet to showcase your pouring skills; this is unnecessary violence and indicates that the beer is naturally not highly carbonated, which is not a significant issue. Similarly, avoid tilting the glass so far that it's almost horizontal, and don't pour the beer so slowly that it produces minimal foam.

The foam's production releases carbon dioxide that would otherwise remain in the beer, leading to uncomfortable bloating when consumed. Therefore, a substantial foam layer is not just aesthetically pleasing but also functionally important.

You can confirm this through personal testing, discovering that beer served correctly is more accessible and enjoyable to drink. From a tasting perspective, it's beneficial to slightly reduce the carbon dioxide level in the glass. An excess of gas on the taste buds is quickly released from the liquid, creating numerous small "explosions." This effect, similar to what happens when beer is excessively cold, numbs the taste buds and reduces their efficiency. Thus, it's important to allow the foam sufficient time to settle and compact itself. Hold the glass vertically as you continue pouring. Wait as needed and, if required, repeat these steps until you achieve the right balance of beer and foam. Naturally, this balance varies depending on the beer style. The photographs accompanying each beer style in the following chapters will provide guidance.

As for those who may not initially appreciate foam, don't worry too much. There's hope in convincing them of the beauty of foam. It can be enjoyable to demonstrate how easy it is to drink beer with a generous head of foam. To avoid swallowing the foam, simply lift and tilt the glass, allowing the beer to flow into your partially open mouth, while the foam politely rests on your upper lip or mustache—assuming you have one.

THE MAJOR COUNTRIES AND THE MAJOR STYLES OF BEER

In this section, we dive into various beer styles, broken down by the countries and regions where they first emerged. It's essential to grasp that while there might be standout beers made by certain brewers, these don't serve as the final representation of a style; every style brings a range of distinct features.

Beer labels and brands, though catchy and distinctive, are essentially the exterior or the "cover." They're vital for identification, but they can be limiting when our goal is more to spark curiosity, pose questions, and propel an endless journey to taste and discover the world's finest beer—which might differ for each person. That's why we've chosen to spotlight beer styles and uncover what's beneath the label, introducing you to the essence and DNA of various beer types.

Styles wrap up a range of traits and objective parameters like color, alcohol content, flavor balance, taste, and aroma. Individual brewers then offer their unique spin on these characteristics. By detailing beer styles, we're giving a nod to their rich history and establishing common ground between the brewer and the drinker.

If you're the type who doesn't like taking a shot in the dark when picking beers, if you're looking to wrap your head around a beer you didn't quite vibe with, or if you're setting out on a "beer hunter" adventure, this style guide is for you. And if you're really into rankings, sites like www.ratebeer.com, www.beeradvocate.com, or www.untappd.com offer loads of opinions. You can even chip in with your own reviews on these beers. But remember, you don't need a certificate to review, just a discerning palate!

In the following pages, you will find details about numerous types of beer, ranging from the most famous to the lesser-known varieties. They are categorized based on the country or region where they are produced. We have consistently used the same categories for each entry, allowing you to make comparisons and create your personal classification. For each beer, we will provide the following information:

FAMILY: This indicates the type of fermentation used, whether it's top fermentation, bottom fermentation, or spontaneous fermentation.

CATEGORY: It identifies the main international family from which the beer style originated.

STYLE: This refers to the particular recipe and production method used, which can vary depending on the geographic area and tradition.

ORIGIN: The country or geographic region from which the beer originates.

For each beer type, we will also provide a brief history, including any unusual or interesting anecdotes, and trace how it evolved to its current form.

PRODUCTION

This section will outline the techniques, ingredients, and perhaps some secrets used in producing the beer in this particular way. For more technical terms, we recommend referring to the glossary.

CHARACTERISTICS

These are the typical elements that distinguish a style of beer. They may be present in varying degrees, depending on the individual brewer's interpretation of the style. This section may not follow a rigid pattern, as it aims to explore various aspects in a more discursive manner. We will attempt to cover a range of characteristics, such as:

Appearance: Describing how the foam and liquid part look, including color and consistency.

Aroma: Identifying the various fragrances perceived through the nose.

Flavor: Discussing the flavors experienced when drinking the beer and the body of the beer.

Mouthfeel: Analyzing the sensations and taste that linger in the mouth after consuming the beer.

Alcohol content: Specifying the amount of alcohol contained in the beer, typically expressed as a percentage by volume.

Pairing: Offering suggestions for traditional, special, or unique food pairings, though experimentation is encouraged. Feel free to explore and enjoy the diverse world of beer!

BELGIUM

Belgium, a country steeped in one of the richest and most enduring brewing traditions, is synonymous with beer. Scattered with breweries and beer gardens, it's the birthplace of Gambrinus, the legendary figure often hailed as the "patron saint" of beer. Over the years, various legends pegged him as the king of Flanders, a server in Charlemagne's court, the pioneer of hop-infused beer, and more.

In the early 1900s, Belgium was home to over 3,300 breweries. However, by the century's end, this number had dwindled to just above 100. But with the new millennium came a revival. Young brewers began experimenting, leading to a resurgence in the brewing industry. Although the heydays of the past might seem distant, smaller producers are now reclaiming market share from the industrial lagers that once dominated Belgian beer aisles. This shift began post-World War II when Belgium countered the global trend of bland, low-alcohol beers by producing rich, high-alcohol ones that maintained the unique spicy yeast notes.

Today's dynamic brewers, like De Ranke in Flanders, De la Senne in Brussels, and La Rulles in Wallonia, are redefining Belgium's beer legacy. Their modern takes, often inspired by long-lost traditional beers, emphasize both hop bitterness and distinct yeast flavors. This revival has also boosted hop cultivation, with

hop farms dotting the landscape with their iconic poles. Moreover, universities are lending a hand, offering microbiology labs to brewers for yeast isolation, ensuring each beer retains a distinctive character.

Belgium's Lambic beers, which almost faded into obscurity, are renowned worldwide. These beers, stemming from age-old brewing methods, faced near extinction due to a shrinking pool of producers and blenders. Today, however, the Lambic sector is booming, especially overseas, even as domestic demand wanes and many traditional Pajottenland cafes shut their doors. Presently, beer enthusiasts flock to places like Moeder Lambic in central Brussels and St Gilles, and de Grote Dorst in Eizeringen. These establishments offer an array of Lambic, Kriek, Gueuze, and other exclusive Belgian beers.

Trappist beers are another staple of the Belgian beer scene. Six monasteries of the Cistercian Order brew beer in Belgium. However, there's often confusion. Some people mistake "Trappist beers" as a beer style, but the "Authentic Trappist Product" label signifies that the beer was brewed within a monastery's walls, overseen by monks. It doesn't imply that a monk was the master brewer. The sales primarily fund charitable works, not the monastery's enrichment.

SAISON

FAMILY: TOP FERMENTATION
CATEGORY: BELGIAN ALE
STYLE: SAISON
ORIGIN: BELGIUM, WALLONIA

Saison beers have historical roots in the farms of Wallonia, the French-speaking region of Belgium. The term "saison" comes from the French word for "season." These beers were initially brewed to quench the thirst of farm laborers during the scorching summer months. They were even partly used as a form of payment. The primary goal was to craft a beer that could withstand the heat of summer while still being refreshing. Historically, these beers had a lower alcohol content. Every farm boasted its unique recipe, which likely evolved based on the available ingredients. In the western regions, particularly northern France, these beers took the place of the higher-alcohol Bières de Garde.

PRODUCTION

Top-fermenting yeasts, adept at functioning at warmer temperatures, help transform the wort into a beer with an alcohol content of 5 to 7% abv. The characteristic spicy notes are often achieved by infusing spices like pepper, cumin, Guinea pepper, coriander, and more. Continental hops are essential for providing both bitterness and aroma. The grain bill might also incorporate wheat and unmalted spelt.

CHARACTERISTICS

Saisons typically sport a pale orange hue, but they can range from a light straw yellow to a deeper amber with copper undertones. Since many aren't filtered, they might have a slightly hazy appearance. The foam is generally abundant, dense, and long-lasting.

The aromatic profile blends the phenolic and spicy scents from the yeast and spices, resulting in a subtle herbal, floral hop bouquet. This aroma is complemented by lingering light malt notes and a crisp citrusy zest.

In terms of flavor, saisons have a medium-light body. Their high carbonation lends a noticeable effervescence. This is matched with a moderately bitter finish and a prolonged aftertaste, which can be zesty, peppered with notes of herbs and lemon. Each brew can vary significantly depending on its producer, but a hallmark of the style is its refreshingly tangy bite.

Alcohol content: 5-7% abv.
Pairing: Perfect with seafood salad and raw vegetable dishes.

BIÈRE BLANCHE

FAMILY: TOP FERMENTATION - WHEAT BEER
CATEGORY: BELGIAN ALE
STYLE: BIÈRE BLANCHE
ORIGIN: BELGIUM

Tracing its roots to the Middle Ages, White Beer or "Bière Blanche" predates the use of hops in brewing. Instead, a mix of herbs known as "gruit" was used for flavor. By the mid-20th century, this beer style was nearly forgotten until Pierre Celis decided to bring it back. Witnessing the closure of the last wheat beer producer in his hometown of Hoegaarden in Flanders, Celis left his job with the mission to resurrect this age-old brew. Today, its refreshing qualities make it a popular choice, especially during the warmer months.

PRODUCTION
This beer is predominantly made with a generous amount of un-malted soft winter wheat, which can make up to half of the cereal composition. Its distinct flavors come from a combination of coriander, bitter orange zest (Curaçao), and a top-fermenting yeast known for its unique aroma profile.

CHARACTERISTICS
Its appearance is a very pale yellow, leaning towards a whitish hue due to the strong cloudiness from the suspended yeast and the inclusion of wheat. This beer showcases a thick, consistent, and lasting white foam.

A gentle honey aroma is complemented by undertones of citrus and spices, which should always remain subtle and not overpowering.

Though medium-light in body, the beer has a well-rounded taste profile. It offers a pronounced flavor intensity but ends with a dry and crisp finish. Its light and invigorating nature makes it a perfect beverage for a summer evening.

Alcohol content: Approximately 5% abv.
Pairing: Ideal with poultry, fish, and shellfish.

BELGIAN GOLDEN STRONG ALE

FAMILY: TOP FERMENTATION
CATEGORY: BELGIAN STRONG ALE
STYLE: BELGIAN GOLDEN STRONG ALE
ORIGIN: BELGIUM

These beers are essentially the non-Trappist version of the Trappist Tripel, created at the Moortgat brewery post-World War II to counter the commercial success of industrially produced lagers. They were attempting to emulate those appealing golden colors. These beers quickly took on "devilish" names and branding, in part as a nod to their founder (in the Flemish dialect, "Duvel" means "devil"), and partly due to their sneaky nature: they look light and innocent, are smooth to drink, but surprise you with a punch of alcohol.

PRODUCTION

Made with Belgian yeast strains that can tolerate high alcohol while emphasizing fruity esters, spicy notes, and fusel alcohols. Pale Pilsner malts provide the color; sugars are added to increase alcohol without adding heaviness, and noble hops are used for aroma.

CHARACTERISTICS

The beer has a lovely golden-yellow hue with abundant foam: a persistent, very white foam that clings to the glass. High carbonation lifts the aromas: fruit (apples, pears, oranges), spices (pepper), and floral hop notes. Flavorful, fruity, spicy notes play nicely with a light maltiness and noticeable bitterness. This bitterness, combined with effervescence and a lighter body, leads to a notably dry finish. It's a complex yet delicate beer style. Deceptively potent!

Alcohol content: about 7.5-10% abv.
Pairing: Grilled red meats.

FLEMISH RED ALE

FAMILY: TOP FERMENTATION (MATURED IN WOOD)
CATEGORY: SOUR ALE
STYLE: FLEMISH RED ALE
ORIGIN: BELGIUM

These traditional beers hail from West Flanders and have been cherished for ages. Their rich hue and unique acidity set them apart, leaning more towards an acetic sharpness than Lambic beers, making them reminiscent of certain wines.

PRODUCTION

Following the primary fermentation, the beer is aged for up to two years in spacious oak barrels. Here, it takes on its tangy nature, courtesy of the natural presence of Brettanomyces, Acetobacteria, and Lactobacillus colonies that gradually modify it. Unlike the process with Lambic beers, there's no "spontaneous fermentation" involved here. The matured beer is then blended with younger batches to harmonize the acidity, adding depth and smoothness to its profile.

CHARACTERISTICS

Boasting a rich Bordeaux hue, verging on a chestnut shade, it draws comparisons to the esteemed wines of Burgundy. The beer is crowned with a medium, lasting foam that varies from white to ivory.

Its aroma is a symphony, harmonizing seamlessly with its taste: deeply fruity, it echoes notes of black cherries, red currants, and plums. Subtle malt undertones bring forth hints of chocolate and a touch of vanilla, while its inherent acidity is gracefully offset by the caramel sweetness of the malt.

This beer is an experience. It beckons an intellectual approach, urging you to appreciate its visual and olfactory charm before diving into its distinctive taste. Even those who might shy away from its tartness will find joy in its sight and scent alone.

Alcohol content: Approximately 4.6-6.5% abv.
Pairing: Ideal as an aperitif, or paired with a cherry tart.

OUD BRUIN OR FLANDERS BROWN

FAMILY: TOP FERMENTATION (MIXED)
CATEGORY: SOUR ALE
STYLE: OUD BRUIN
ORIGIN: BELGIUM

Closely akin to the Flemish Red Ale, but hailing from East Flanders, the "Old Browns" boast a richer hue, a throwback to times when perfectly roasting malts was trickier. An extended boil over direct flame would often caramelize the sugars. This results in a less tart profile than its western counterpart, with the malt's sweetness harmonizing the beer's sour notes.

PRODUCTION
This beer matures extensively, not in wood but in stainless steel tanks at room temperature. Its tanginess is amplified by adding lactic bacteria or acidulated malts, along with carbonate and magnesium-rich water.

CHARACTERISTICS
Sporting a chestnut shade with hints of red, its aroma is robust and intricate. Notes of caramel, toffee, chocolate, and a medley of ripe and dried fruits (black cherries, prunes, figs, dates, and raisins) come through. It's less acetic than the Flemish Red Ale. This beer, while more direct, still calls for a receptive palate and curiosity.

Alcohol content: Ranges from 5-8% abv.
Pairing: Best with game and venison.

DUBBEL AND TRIPEL

FAMILY: TOP FERMENTATION
CATEGORY: BELGIAN STRONG ALE
STYLE: DUBBEL AND TRIPEL
ORIGIN: BELGIUM

Dubbel and Tripel, despite their misleading names implying double or triple fermentation or malt, trace back to the Trappist abbey of Westmalle. The abbey brews three varieties: a low-alcohol beer for in-house consumption, a mid-tier with roasted malts, and a potent brew. They're distinguished by single, double, or triple X markings on their barrels, leading to the names: Extra, Dubbel, and Tripel.

PRODUCTION

The ingredients encompass water, a mix of barley malts (with Dubbel also using toasted and caramelized types, and Tripel opting for basic and aromatic ones), European hops, often candi or white sugar (to up the alcohol content without altering the body), and, crucially, top-fermenting yeast. In true Belgian fashion, they undergo rigorous bottle re-fermentation.

CHARACTERISTICS

Dubbel, with an alcohol content between 6 and 7.5% abv, varies in color from amber to deep copper and is topped with a creamy, lasting foam head. Its aromatic profile, redolent of fruits and toffee, results from the synergy between malts and yeasts. Its medium body harmonizes with its alcoholic warmth.

Tripel, which packs between 7.5 and 9.5% abv, flaunts a clear, vibrant golden hue, complemented by a thick, lingering foam. Its aroma is a blend of spice and fruit (notably citrus, apricot or apricot jam, and occasionally banana), with a slight floral hop note. These beers epitomize the balance between malts and yeasts, their dryness belies their high alcoholic punch.

Pairing: Both Dubbel and Tripel are sublime with cheese and are equally delightful with carbonade flamande or a hearty game stew.

LAMBIC

FAMILY: SPONTANEOUS FERMENTATION
CATEGORY: LAMBIC
STYLE: LAMBIC
ORIGIN: BELGIUM - PAJOTTENLAND

Lambic beers originate from a region stretching from Brussels along the River Senne, through Pajottenland. This region has a high concentration of wild yeasts, particularly from the Brettanomyces family. This allows brewers to still produce spontaneously fermented beers without adding yeast, just letting nature do its thing. Traditional brewers typically produce this beer during the colder months, roughly from October to late March.

PRODUCTION
Ingredients include water, malted barley, 40% un-malted wheat, and aged hops that have lost their bitterness and aroma but still have preservative qualities. The wort is cooled overnight in an open, wide, shallow tank, then transferred to usually reused barrels where it ferments and matures, from one to four years.

CHARACTERISTICS
Lambics range from pale yellow to gold in color, often slightly hazy and typically foamless. Aromas can remind you of a cellar (like old playing cards, leather, horse saddles) combined with citrusy notes. Older versions may also have fruity (apple) and honey undertones. They're tart in taste with a light body, making them quite drinkable. A Lambic is an acquired taste but can be incredibly refreshing once you grow to like it. It's not just beer, it's Lambic!

Alcoholic content: about 5-6% abv.
Pairing: Quality salami.

Some Lambic versions also have fruit additions like cherries, raspberries, grapes, peaches, or blackcurrants (as shown on the right). They are bottle-fermented and often blend various fruit Lambics of different ages, similar to Gueuze blending. Gueuze itself (shown on the left) is bottle-fermented, made by blending young Lambic with one or more older Lambics aged two to three years.

ENGLAND

England stands tall as one of the nations with a deep-rooted and significant brewing heritage, evidenced by numerous historical records and archaeological finds. Interestingly, the term "Ale," which broadly refers to all beers produced using top-fermenting yeasts today, can trace its origins to the Old English word "ealu." This grain-based beverage was mentioned as early as the 8th century in the renowned Anglo-Saxon epic, Beowulf.

A pivotal shift in beer production occurred during the Middle Ages when King Henry VIII sought to undermine the Catholic Church's influence by dissolving monasteries and convents, effectively stripping them of their brewing privileges. From that point on, the abbey beer tradition remained only on mainland Europe. In England, laypeople—often women—took the helm of barley fermentation, even at household levels. England's brewers always held the raw ingredients in higher regard than the brewing methods, which are notably straightforward, efficient, and logical.

Historically, English brewers understood how to "adjust" their water for optimal beer production. Recognizing that beers like the London Bitter thrived when brewed in Burton-on-Trent, they sought to uncover the reason. They found it in Burton-on-Trent's gypsum-rich waters. Thus, London brewers began adding gypsum to their water to mirror Burton's profile, a practice now globally known as Burtonization. Consequently, many London brewers zealously protect their recipes, often encoding them to signify the specific water adjustments.

Moreover, the English pioneered barley cultivation research, introducing strains custom-selected for particular brews. They delved into malting processes like Maris Otter and Golden Promise, named after their specific barley types—both of which are Pale malts. And while hops solidified their place post-1500, England's hop heritage is illustrious. Iconic strains like Fuggle and Golding have shaped English beer, laying the foundation for numerous new hybrids. Thanks to pioneering efforts from institutions like Wye College in Kent, which operated under London University and then Imperial College until its 2009 closure, we have a wealth of knowledge on hops, driving innovations from the US to New Zealand.

Today's English beers—exclusively top-fermented—are seemingly crafted for leisurely consumption by the gallon in public houses or the renowned "pubs." Here, the characteristically reserved Brits slowly shed their restraint, pint after pint, mingling and connecting. Even now, pub-goers relish cellar-temperature bitters, porters, milds, and brown ales. These are dispensed from hand pumps, sans CO_2 propulsion, and paired with traditional meals or quick bites. While pubs remain quintessential spaces for drinks and camaraderie, they might not always win culinary accolades.

It's noteworthy that traditional Anglo-Saxon beers persist, in large part due to the efforts of the volunteer-run CAMRA (CAMpaign for Real Ale). This body ardently advocates for the preservation of genuine English ales, the Real Ales. Their relentless campaigns have spurred pubs to become "free houses," liberated from brewery ties, granting them the liberty to curate their beer offerings.

ENGLISH BARLEY WINE

FAMILY: TOP FERMENTATION
CATEGORY: STRONG ALE
STYLE: ENGLISH BARLEY WINE
ORIGIN: ENGLAND

English Barley Wines rank among the most alcoholic and full-bodied of English Ales. Opulent, intricate, and captivating, they boast a richness in malt and hops. They possess such a longevity that it's a tradition for brewers to label both the production year and the suggested consumption date. In countries where such labeling is mandatory, these dates hold symbolic importance. It's not unusual to find labels whimsically suggesting, "Best consumed before the end of the world!"

The term "Barley Wine" emerged at the cusp of the 19th and 20th centuries. Originally, it didn't denote a particular style; instead, it signaled the brewery's strongest beer. Bass Brewery pioneered this terminology with their Strong Ale No. 1. However, the legacy of brewing potent beers has ancient roots, tracing back to the old March beers crafted at each season's close.

CHARACTERISTICS

These ales incorporate a medley of malts, bittering English hops like Target, and yeast strains with a high alcohol tolerance. After an extensive fermentation process, they undergo a significant rest period, sometimes maturing in wooden barrels reminiscent of olden practices. Their hues span from pale amber to brown but never approach pitch black. Typically, they feature mild carbonation, with foam being a subtle presence. In contrast, their aroma is pronounced, presenting ethereal notes of honey, fruit (especially dried varieties), caramel, toffee, and molasses. Freshly brewed versions prominently display hop aromas, which mellow over time, giving way to vinous undertones akin to port and sherry. Tasting these beers unveils a full, almost tactile body, accentuated by the multifaceted sweetness of malts, dried fruit hints, hop bitterness, and a spicy zing. They conclude with a prolonged, satisfying finish and a warming alcohol sensation rather than a sharp burn.

In stark contrast to Bitter beers, a single glass of Barley Wine could be your sole companion on a chilly winter evening, ideally paired with an engrossing book by the fireside.

Alcohol content: Approximately 8-13% abv.
Pairing: Perfect for contemplative sipping on its own, this beer also pairs wonderfully with robust blue cheeses or those with a spicy kick.

ENGLISH IPA

FAMILY: TOP FERMENTATION
CATEGORY: INDIA PALE ALE (IPA)
STYLE: ENGLISH IPA
ORIGIN: ENGLAND

The English IPA is a traditionally hop-forward beer currently enjoying a resurgence in various countries. While its popularity may be waning slightly in its homeland, its reputation has skyrocketed among beer enthusiasts and brewers, thanks in part to the infusion of contemporary aromatic hops. While it might not appeal to all palates, it's arguably at the pinnacle of its acclaim.

Dating back to the late 18th century, the India Pale Ale (or IPA) was initially the robust March beer exported to India, earning its name from this practice. Its notable alcohol content and generous hopping ensured it weathered the extended sea voyage well. When the 19th century brought tax hikes that shut many English brewers out of the critical Russian market, they pivoted to the burgeoning Indian market. Here, they exported beers resembling their traditional ones but with a paler, lighter hue, aligning with the prevailing trends. The Burton-on-Trent Pale Ales, which were well-attenuated, slightly more alcoholic, and generously hopped, became the gold standard for the IPA style. Soon after, they gained popularity back home, known simply as Pale Ales.

CHARACTERISTICS

Modern IPAs are somewhat lighter in hue, ranging from gold to amber, crowned by a fine, enduring, and compact foam. Their flavor profile leans heavily on hops, often employing dry-hopping during maturation to fine-tune their aromatic bouquet, spanning floral, spicy, herbal, and resinous notes. However, any bitterness in the finish should be smooth, not harsh. The malt presence and the beer's body should be discernible, ensuring a harmonious flavor balance.

With their distinct and captivating hop-forward character, these beers can both surprise and enchant with their vivid hop notes.

Alcohol volume: Typically 5-7.5% abv.
Pairing: Pairs exceptionally well with spicy and hot dishes of various cuisines.

ORDINARY BITTER

FAMILY: TOP FERMENTATION
CATEGORY: ENGLISH PALE ALE
STYLE: ORDINARY BITTER (OR SIMPLY BITTER)
ORIGIN: ENGLAND (LONDON)

Bitters are ales that, as the name implies, can taste bitter. However, in today's diverse landscape of beer styles, they aren't extraordinarily bitter, especially when juxtaposed with the sharper and more pronounced bitterness of styles like the India Pale Ale. Historically, the term "Bitter" emerged in the 19th century to highlight that these ales were notably hoppy, making them bitterer than the prevalent beers of the era, namely Porters and Milds. Another distinguishing factor was their color. After centuries of brown beers, the outcome of using brown malts roasted on wood fires, these ales were "paler" or amber in color. This shift in hue was due to the use of malts dried using contemporary techniques, leading to the alternate name "Pale Ale." This nomenclature led to some confusion, with some referring to bottled versions as Pale Ales, while the casked counterpart was dubbed Bitter Ale. Such overlap between Bitters and Pale Ales shouldn't cause any concern.

Historically, Bitters were categorized by their alcohol content and structure, with variants like Best Bitter, Special Bitter, Extra Special Bitter, and Strong Bitter. What's essential today, however, is recognizing the modern interpretations crafted by independent brewers, which may differ from the traditional "Real Ale" style.

CHARACTERISTICS
Ordinary Bitters are the mildest and most straightforward of the family. They are all top-fermented, typically showcasing a golden to amber hue, coupled with a balanced and inviting aroma. Their flavor profile boasts malt (with hints of caramel) and fresh hops (floral, resinous, and spicy, characteristic of Kent), accompanied by the fruity undertones from yeast esters. Their light body and subtly bitter finish make them remarkably drinkable.

Regarded as England's quintessential "session beer," Bitters are best enjoyed fresh and served at cellar temperatures, preferably straight from a pump or cask in a cozy pub.

Alcohol content: Typically 3-3.5% abv.
Pairing: Ideal with good friends in a welcoming pub, paired with roast chicken and potatoes—or simply another pint of Bitter.

BROWN PORTER

FAMILY: TOP FERMENTATION
CATEGORY: PORTER
STYLE: BROWN PORTER
ORIGIN: ENGLAND

Brown Porter is a dark ale that has its roots in the Brown Ales of 18th-century London. Its initial success was so profound that it was enveloped in myths and legends from its inception. Legend has it that the working-class patrons of the time would frequent pubs and order a "three threads"—a pint composed of one-third cheap light beer, another third of a robust and pricier "ale," and the final third being the coveted "twopenny," which they couldn't afford in full. However, this mix-and-match approach was a hassle for publicans, slowing down service and frustrating other customers. To streamline the process, an inventive publican decided to pre-mix these three beers. This concoction eventually earned the name "Porter" due to its immense popularity among port workers and laborers.

While this tale is engaging, the reality is different. Porter was the pioneer in industrial-scale beer production—affordable, mass-produced, and sold "ready to drink," distinguishing itself from other beers that matured in pub cellars. Yet, after nearly three centuries of success, Porter's allure waned, being deemed "lowbrow," and eventually eclipsed by the more potent Stout.

Porters are typically deep brown with dark red tints, topped with medium-lasting, cream-colored foam. The predominant flavor is roasted malt, smooth and mild without any burnt undertones, complemented by hints of caramel, coffee, and chocolate. American versions tend to emphasize hops more than their English counterparts, in terms of both bitterness and aroma. Its medium-light body and excellent attenuation make it a user-friendly dark ale.

The Brown Porter stands as the more modest counterpart in the Porter family, being lighter and more refined than the Robust Porter and Baltic (or Imperial) Porter.

Alcohol content: Typically 4-5.4% abv.
Pairing: Ideal with braised beef or beef stew that's been marinated in Porter.

MILD

FAMILY: TOP FERMENTATION
CATEGORY: ENGLISH BROWN ALE
STYLE: MILD
ORIGIN: ENGLAND

Historically, the term "Mild" described beers sold "fresh," meaning they were recently brewed without undergoing the lengthy maturation typical of Old Ales, which softened their flavors. After World War I, "Mild" came to represent lighter, more affordable beers, aligning with the era's austerity. These brews were mainstays in English pubs until after World War II, after which they lost ground to the lighter and crisper Pale Ales.

Nowadays, this beer style garners little interest beyond a niche of beer aficionados. Recognizing its dwindling popularity, the English CAMRA (Campaign for Real Ale) association launched a "Save the Mild" campaign, symbolically dubbing May as "Mild Month." During this month, local CAMRA branches encourage pubs to feature at least one Mild on their beer menu and organize special tasting events to champion Milds. This initiative underscores the precarious position of this beer style in a market now enamored with hop-forward brews.

CHARACTERISTICS

Milds span a color range from dark brown (nearing black) to amber. Their profiles can vary—some come across as dark ales with a wintry vibe, flaunting roasted and caramelized notes, while others are lighter, offering refreshing and quenching qualities suitable for pairing with a variety of dishes.

Unified by their low alcohol content and medium-light body, Milds primarily showcase malty sweetness. Some might have a subtle hop presence, both aromatically and in flavor. Occasional hints of diacetyl might also appear. Since Milds don't typically excel in bottled form, they're best enjoyed from a draft.

Alcohol content: Below 4.3% abv.
Pairing: Milds pair excellently with white cream cheeses and both sheep and goat cheeses. The cheeses' mild acidity contrasts beautifully with the sweetness and maltiness of the beer.

RUSSIAN IMPERIAL STOUT

FAMILY: TOP FERMENTATION
CATEGORY: STOUT
STYLE: RUSSIAN IMPERIAL STOUT
ORIGIN: ENGLAND

Russian Imperial Stouts are the boldest and most robust within the Stout category. The "Russian" label recalls these Ales' immense popularity at the Russian tsars' court in the 19th century. The Russian market, along with those of the Baltic countries, was a significant export destination for these brews.

Every ingredient in this beer is generously employed, resulting in a complex blend of flavors. They're exceptionally dark, verging on an opaque black, attributed to the comprehensive use of dark roasted malts. The aroma boasts potent hop notes, culminating in a bitter finish where hop bitterness intertwines with the depth of the dark malts.

CHARACTERISTICS

These beers captivate with their aromatic profile, derived from yeasts that produce pronounced fruity esters reminiscent of stewed plums, sultanas, and other dried fruits and nuts. Boasting high alcohol content, these stouts are full-bodied, intense, and intricately layered. One could liken them to the darker, more mysterious siblings of Barley Wine. Their flavor profile lingers, leaving a lasting impression on the palate. Modern versions brewed in the United States push the envelope even further.

Approaching a Russian Imperial Stout demands an educated palate and some familiarity with robust brews. But for those who love a challenge and are ready to take the plunge, the experience can be transformative. If you can navigate through the deep, intricate layers of this beer, you might find yourself utterly enchanted.

Alcohol content: Approximately 8-12% abv.
Pairing: A slice of chocolate pudding or a cup of rich coffee.

IRELAND

reland boasts a brewing legacy that stands shoulder-to-shoulder with the traditions of other Anglo-Saxon nations. Yet, for many, the mere mention of Ireland evokes the iconic image of a dark, full pint with creamy foam, perhaps garnished with a clover leaf traced on its surface. While one must tip their hat to the Irish, it's crucial to acknowledge that Stout's birthplace was London. However, it was Arthur Guinness and his renowned brewery that catapulted Stout to global acclaim. Now, any conversation about Dublin inevitably involves references to both James Joyce and the emblematic golden harp featured on all Guinness merchandise.

Established in 1759, the Guinness company has been at the forefront of brewing innovations. They pioneered the method of dispensing beer using a blend of carbon dioxide and nitrogen. This technique ensures the beer fills the glass without over-carbonation, yielding its signature creamy foam. In striving for consistency, even their cans and bottles contain mechanisms to replicate the pub experience.

Unlike Britain — a bubbling cauldron of brewing creativity, reimagined beer styles, and the frequent birth of new pubs and breweries — Ireland takes pride in its time-honored brewing traditions. Even in the face of economic challenges, Ireland's beer consumption remains steadfast. It's a testament to the nation's resilience and passion for its brews. As the storm clouds of economic downturns pass, one can be optimistic that Irish breweries will emerge stronger, potentially embracing innovation once again.

For now, whether nestled in bustling cities or quaint villages amidst verdant landscapes, traditional Irish pubs stand as cultural touchstones. Here, patrons can savor pints of Irish Red Ale, perhaps while delving into James Joyce's *Dubliners*, envisioning the historical tapestry of Dublin, or cheering for the national rugby team, clad in their emblematic green jerseys.

IRISH RED ALE

FAMILY: TOP FERMENTATION
CATEGORY: IRISH AND SCOTCH ALE
STYLE: IRISH RED ALE
ORIGIN: IRELAND

While Stout originated in London, the Irish Red Ale captures the true essence of Irish brewing. It emerged as a counterpoint to the extra special bitter beers of the island. It boasts a higher alcohol content than many beers from London and its surrounding areas and has a flavor profile that emphasizes malt over hops.

PRODUCTION

Irish Reds are brewed with a generous amount of malts, whether local or English, often incorporating Caramel and occasionally Roasted varieties. The yeast's character isn't especially pronounced, but there's a noticeable buttery hint (diacetyl) which, in small amounts, is quite appealing. English hops are also used, but sparingly; they often take a backseat since Roasted malts are preferred to provide bitterness. Some versions are even bottom-fermented.

CHARACTERISTICS

Its color is a clear amber, accented with coppery highlights and typically topped with a white head. On the nose, dominant aromas of caramel and toffee come through, sometimes joined by toasted undertones. The scents from yeast and hops are either subdued or overshadowed by the malt aromas. The beer has a medium body with moderate carbonation. In terms of flavor, sweet caramel and malt-induced bitterness are prevalent, often paired with a "roasted" nuance that's heightened by a dry finish. When sipped, these flavors meld with delightful toasted buttery notes attributed to the yeast.

These beers are very drinkable and are a good choice at any time of the day, especially the lighter alcohol versions.

Alcohol content: Roughly 4-6% ABV.
Pairing: They pair exceptionally well with traditional Irish meat dishes.

DRY STOUT

FAMILY: TOP FERMENTATION
CATEGORY: STOUT
STYLE: DRY STOUT
ORIGIN: ENGLAND/IRELAND

Originally crafted to satisfy the thirst of London pub-goers after the success of Porters, these beers were initially the boozier siblings and dubbed "Stout Porters." Their current, milder alcohol content owes much to the iconic Irish breweries: Arthur Guinness, Beamish, and Murphy's. Today, the Dry Stouts relished in Dublin and nearby areas have become rarities worldwide, almost vanishing in London.

Though challenging to find in bottles, they're readily available on tap, which is the recommended way to enjoy them.

PRODUCTION
Roasted, yet un-malted, barley imparts both the distinct color and dry character to these beers. Occasionally, barley flakes — never malted — are included to enhance their creaminess. The primary grist comprises Pale malts. English hops, a crucial component, lend the beer its bitterness. Ideally, the water should be soft, and the yeast's attenuation is vital in accentuating the beer's dryness.

CHARACTERISTICS
These stouts boast a dark and often opaque hue, crowned by a consistent, creamy foam reminiscent of cappuccino. Their aroma weaves notes of barley, chocolate, cocoa beans, and carob, sometimes tinged with fruity undertones from the yeast. They possess a body that's somewhere between medium-light and medium-full. Moderate carbonation, occasionally paired with a mild acidity, counterbalances the dry, bitter finish, which lingers with hints of molten chocolate and coffee.

Alcohol content: Approximately 4-5% ABV.
Pairing: Despite their lower alcohol content, they wonderfully complement fatty dishes, including smoked and grilled items, smoked cheeses, pastries, and coffee-infused desserts.

SCOTLAND

S cotland is famous for its whiskies, in particular for the peaty, Islay styles, rather than for its brewing tradition. In that whisky is the distillation of a cereal fermentation (in practice a beer made with a yeast specially chosen by the distilleries), without beer these distillations would not exist; and indeed the Scots are not adverse to drinking a pint of beer.

The Scots have a reputation for thrift, and instead of giving names to the styles of beer, they have simply categorized them according to how much they cost: from 60, 70, 80 or 90 shillings, a term that has survived even after the disappearance of the shilling when the currency was decimalized. The 90 is also known as Scotch Ale or Wee Heavy, being the most alcoholic (up to 10%), but the most commonly drunk are the session beers, namely the 60 and 70 (with an alcohol content between 2.5% and 3.9%).

Probably again for economic reasons, their beers are characterized by malts (locally produced) rather than by hops that would have to be imported from England. The result are beers with a much stronger taste of malt and a fuller body, as well as being darker than their English cousins.

Scotland is experiencing a great brewing renaissance thanks to the enterprise of BrewDog, a non-conformist brewer par excellence. It has reinterpreted the traditional beers and offered new ones, inspired by the Anglo-American school or without any links with the past. The brilliant marketing used to publicize its products or simply to attract attention is sometimes criticized for its excesses (as in the case of the beer called The End of the History with an alcohol content of 55%, sold in bottles contained in stuffed squirrels); but it undoubtedly has a strong media impact. Under its influence the whole of Scotland is rapidly rewriting its own brewing history.

STRONG SCOTCH ALE

FAMILY: TOP FERMENTATION
CATEGORY: IRISH AND SCOTCH ALE
STYLE: STRONG SCOTCH ALE OR WEE HEAVY
ORIGIN: SCOTLAND

Scotch ales epitomize traditional Scottish brewing. Due to the challenges and expense of importing hops from the southern parts of the British Isles, these beers primarily use barley malts grown in Scotland. They're a staple in pubs from bustling cities like Glasgow and Edinburgh to quaint, remote villages. Historically priced by shilling categories, Scotch ales come in varieties of 60, 70, and 80 shillings (also termed Scottish Light, Heavy, and Export) with alcohol content between 2.5% and 5% abv. The 90-shilling variety, widely recognized as (Strong) Scotch Ale or Wee Heavy, boasts the highest alcohol content and price.

PRODUCTION

Apart from a significant amount of Pale malts, the mixture typically comprises Roasted and Crystal malts. These are added more for color than sweetness, often derived from the caramelization process during mashing. Occasionally, brewers incorporate small quantities of malts smoked with diverse woods or peat. Given hops' English roots, they're sparingly used in these brews.

CHARACTERISTICS

These ales showcase colors from amber to deep brown, akin to a monk's robe, topped with frothy, cappuccino-like foam. The aroma combines yeast's esters and alcohol (more pronounced in the higher-alcohol versions) with undertones of caramel, earth, and occasionally, smoky peat. Flavor profiles hint at prunes, raisins, and other dried fruits. With body ranging from medium to full (sometimes even viscous) and moderate carbonation, these beers strike a balance despite their inherent sweetness, ending with a dry, slightly charred finish.

Alcohol content: about 6.5-10% abv.
Pairing: Ideal with meat dishes, including lamb, and for the smokier, peaty variants, strong or blue cheeses.

GERMANY

Germany boasts an ancient brewing tradition, yet it's also credited for introducing the world to modern Pale Lager beers, thanks to techniques honed in its industrial breweries. Despite the Bavarian Purity Law—which was enforced across all states of the federation until the late 20th century—Germany has crafted an array of beer varieties, including some that sidestep this law. This diversity stems from Germany's tapestry of tiny principalities, each holding onto its own laws and traditions. Consequently, every town and region possesses a unique beer heritage.

In Bavaria, one encounters the iconic wheat beers: Weissbier (or "white beer") and Weizenbier (or "wheat beer"). They're distinguished by the yeast's phenol and the robust presence of wheat malt. There's also the Hell-style beer, a paragon of simplicity, standing in contrast to the Märzen beers, which flow generously during Munich's annual Oktoberfest. This festival, pausing only for wars or significant catastrophes, resembles a vast amusement park. Its grand structures house the city's breweries and draw millions, including a vast number of international tourists.

Journeying a bit further north, the age-old tradition of Zoigl beers thrives. Crafted by select families with historic brewing rights, these beers emerge from the town's shared brewery. Often, they're sold right from the brewer's home, which might transform into a makeshift pub, or from special venues resembling a "Gasthaus"—essentially an inn or tavern offering meals.

Beyond Munich, cities like Dortmund have imprinted their distinct marks on beer styles. Dortmund, for instance, presents Dortmunder, their answer to the Hell and Pils styles.

Cologne stands out with a powerful brewing legacy, arguably diverging from the national trend. Its signature Kölsch—a top-fermented, pale, and clear beer with modest alcohol content—can only be crafted within the city confines. Typically, it's relished directly in brewery-adjacent pubs, often poured right from the barrel, its subdued carbonation making for easy serving.

A stone's throw from Cologne, Düsseldorf beckons with its Alt beers—top-fermented and amber-hued. These beers draw and captivate aficionados. One of the city's main streets is adorned with time-honored breweries offering just this beverage and its potent winter variant. Here, patrons can savor traditional meals paired with this low-alcohol, slightly toasted beer.

Nearby, Bonn offers its Bonsch beer, seemingly an understated answer to its Cologne and Dusseldorf counterparts.

In Berlin, especially in the areas that once constituted East Germany, traditional beers face threats from more lucrative commercial counterparts. Berliner Weiss clings on, currently witnessing a quiet renaissance, thanks to international brewers championing its cause. In the capital, one can still savor these mildly sour beers, often tempered with woodruff or other fruit syrups. Further south, in Leipzig, Gose beers, originally from Goslar, are

staging a comeback. These distinct beers, brewed with saline water, wheat, and coriander, have now garnered global admiration.

Franconia, the northern tip of Bavaria, emerges as a haven for beer enthusiasts. Here, familial brewers uphold age-old recipes, crafting beers in annexes behind their taverns. In Bamberg—dubbed the brewing capital and an unscathed relic from World War II's bombings—historic breweries abound. This city gave birth to Rauchbier, the smoky brews that are now replicated and revered globally. Depending on the season, locals in these brewery-taverns consume varying beers like Fasten (Easter beers), Märzen, Bock, Doppelbock, Keller Bier, Land Bier, and Ungespundet. These masterpieces, in all their simplicity, offer distinct experiences.

In smaller hamlets, with maybe just one brewery, locals have limited choices. However, where multiple breweries exist, it's traditional for families to patronize just one—a choice made generations ago. Come summer, larger breweries unveil their Biergarten, or open-air bars, while smaller ones supply their brews to independent establishments. These spots become evening (and often afternoon) hubs for locals to bask in the sun and beer alike.

Germany's rich tradition extends to brewing schools, barley and hop cultivation, and malting, forming a premier-quality production chain. While the Purity Law might have curtailed brewers' creativity, fostering conservatism, recent times signal change. Alongside the traditional noble hops, new aromatic variants are surfacing—Europe's answer to the New World's continuous innovations. Some local brewers even incorporate American hop types, crafting less conventional beer styles and intriguing younger beer aficionados. Encouragingly, hops grown in Hallertau, a premier cultivation area, seem better suited for local beers than their North American counterparts.

MÜNCHNER HELL

FAMILY: BOTTOM FERMENTATION
CATEGORY: LIGHT LAGER
STYLE: MÜNCHNER HELL
ORIGIN: GERMANY (MUNICH)

Hell beers originated at the Spaten brewery in Munich in the late 19th century, designed as a response to the burgeoning popularity of Bohemian Pils beers. These beers aimed to mimic the pale golden yellow hue of the Bohemian beers, achieved using German Pils malt, and their herbaceous notes, which were derived from native hops. The distinguishing characteristic of Hell beers is their pronounced malt sweetness, which takes precedence over hop bitterness—they use about half the hops of a Bohemian Pils.

In German, the term "Hell" inherently suggests "beer" and simply denotes a "light beer."

PRODUCTION

Creating such a pristine, straightforward beer demands a keen focus on the quality of the ingredients. For Münchner Hell, and perhaps even more than for other bottom-fermented beers, maintaining a low fermentation temperature and ensuring extended cold maturation are essential to prevent the emergence of fruity esters.

CHARACTERISTICS

Münchner Hell offers a medium-bodied, smooth, and rounded profile, consistently well-balanced and never cloying. This balance is achieved thanks to a measured, expert use of hops that subtly complement and elevate the malt profile.

Evoking feelings of nostalgia, this beer is akin to a familiar, comforting presence—a timeless classic that's hard to decline.

Alcohol content: Approximately 4.7-5.4%.
Pairing: It pairs beautifully with light fare, but also holds its own against the fiery kick of spicy curried sausage.

MÜNCHNER DUNKEL

FAMILY: BOTTOM FERMENTATION
CATEGORY: DARK LAGER
STYLE: MÜNCHNER DUNKEL
ORIGIN: SOUTHERN GERMANY

Münchner Dunkels, while less renowned and less prevalent than their modern counterparts, the Münchner Hell, are truly the progenitors of the style. These are the original lagers of southern Bavaria, stored in the coolness of caves since the 1500s. It is believed that these beers employed naturally selected bottom-fermenting yeasts, which were later isolated by Hansen. Traditionally, they contained minimal hop content, given southern Bavaria's distance from the central hop trade in the northern cities of the Hanseatic League, and also due to the use of "gruit."

In German, "Dunkel" translates to "dark."

PRODUCTION

Münchner Dunkel is customarily brewed using 100% Munich malt, undergoing an extended decoction. This process results in the caramelization of the sugars, further accentuating the color and flavor of the malt.

CHARACTERISTICS

Boasting a distinctive brown to garnet-red hue with a thick, creamy head, these beers exude a robust aroma characteristic of Munich's amber malts, featuring caramel and toasted bread notes. They offer a full, yet not overpowering body, with the sweetness and intricacy of the malts taking center stage, subtly accented by hints of toasted flavors and noble hops.

When in Bavaria, it's worth seeking out unfiltered versions crafted by local artisanal brewers—a genuine trip back in time. And don't let the deep color deter you!

Alcohol content: Approximately 4.5-5.6% ABV.
Pairing: Grilled salamella (sausage).

MÄRZEN/OKTOBERFEST

FAMILY: BOTTOM FERMENTATION
CATEGORY: EUROPEAN AMBER LAGER
STYLE: MÄRZEN/OKTOBERFEST
ORIGIN: GERMANY (MUNICH)

Before modern refrigeration, März (German for "March") was the last month suitable for brewing beer due to the impending warmth of spring and summer. Warm conditions not only stressed the yeast but also invited bacteria, affecting the beer's quality. While medieval brewers might not have understood microbiology, they recognized that the cooler conditions of autumn and winter produced superior brews. Caves became essential for storing ice collected during the winter, along with the beer, to replicate these cooler brewing conditions. As a result, March was a busy month for brewers. The goal was not only to stockpile beer for the warm months but also to utilize the remaining hops and malt before the new harvest and brewing season. The malt-rich Märzen beers, with their slightly elevated alcohol content and abundant hop flavor, were particularly suitable for this prolonged storage.

By the time October arrived, brewing resumed, and the barrels storing Märzen needed emptying. This necessity birthed the tradition of communal festivities to consume the matured beers. Over the months, these beers would have developed a pronounced malt character, with diminished bitterness and hop aromas.

This evolution of Märzen beers offers a credible backstory to their malt-forward taste and to the age-old Oktoberfest traditions. However, the modern Oktoberfest has its roots in the nuptials of Prince Ludwig and Princess Therese of Saxony on October 12, 1810. Munich's residents celebrated on a space known as Theresienwiese, which still hosts the world's largest beer festival. Only six premier Munich breweries can serve beer at this grand event.

CHARACTERISTICS
Märzen/Oktoberfest beers exhibit an enticing orangey, reddish-gold hue. They stand out as one of the most refined malt-forward styles—smooth, intricate, and graceful. While Märzen is brewed in March, its prime is in October, hence the call for the hearty one-liter tankard (equivalent to a US quart).

Alcohol content: Approximately 4.8-5.7% ABV.
Pairing: Ideal with shin and pretzel or roast pork accompanied by
sauce chasseur and boiled potato dumplings.

SCHWARZBIER

FAMILY: BOTTOM FERMENTATION
CATEGORY: DARK LAGER
STYLE: SCHWARZBIER
ORIGIN: GERMANY

Derived from the German term meaning "black beer," Schwarzbier, sometimes referred to as a black Pils, presents a somewhat misleading name. While it might be the darkest among lagers, most examples aren't entirely opaque black, unless viewed through an especially wide glass.

The origins of Schwarzbier remain disputed. Some speculate that it emerged inspired by the popular English Porter beers, while others suggest it could be an offshoot of the Münchner Dunkel.

CHARACTERISTICS

Schwarzbier's elegant, dark brown hue is enlivened by ruby and bright brick-red undertones. It's topped with abundant, cappuccino-colored foam. Despite its dark appearance, the aroma is pleasantly delicate, featuring hints of roasted coffee, seamlessly balanced by malty undertones, all while avoiding any fruity ester presence. On tasting, it doesn't present as overly sharp, scorched, or bitter. Instead, flavors of coffee, chocolate, and vanilla come through, all accompanied by the characteristic German malt sweetness. Its hop profile remains subdued, both in bitterness and aroma, but makes a gentle appearance towards the finish, which leans dry without fully committing to it.

Sporting a medium-light body, ample carbonation, and moderate alcohol content, Schwarzbier offers a welcoming introduction to the world of dark beers. Sampling a high-quality Schwarzbier might be a game-changer, dispelling any preconceived notions about lagers or dark beers.

Alcohol content: Approximately 4.4-5.4% ABV.
Pairing: Ideally complements grilled salmon trout, especially those savored at the Annafest in Forchheim towards July's end.

TRADITIONAL BOCK

FAMILY: BOTTOM FERMENTATION
CATEGORY: BOCK
STYLE: TRADITIONAL BOCK
ORIGIN: GERMANY

The name "Bock" traces its origins to the city of Heinbeck in Lower Saxony, a renowned hub for trade and beer production during the Hanseatic League era. As these beers journeyed south to Bavaria, the name "Heinbeck" morphed into "Bock" in the local dialect, which also means "goat." This dual meaning is often depicted with goat imagery on the beer labels.

PRODUCTION
Traditional Bock is a testament to the amber malts like Munich and Vienna, which find a splendid representation in this brew. The use of continental hops is minimal, serving only to temper the malty sweetness that characterizes a Bock's finish.

CHARACTERISTICS
While Bocks were historically brown, contemporary variants lean towards amber and copper hues. However, their brilliance remains consistent, attributed to prolonged aging, and they're crowned with a persistent, fine, compact foam. Both the aroma and taste are dominated by the malt's rich, full-bodied complexity, complemented by the discernible presence of alcohol, adding depth to the experience.

Alcohol content: Approximately 6.3-7.2% ABV.
Pairing: Complements smoked meat carpaccio perfectly.

In the Bock family, there are also the clearer, dry-hopped Maibock; the more challenging elder sisters, Doppelbock (with an alcohol content of up to 10%); and the extreme Eisbock. This last type can reach very high alcohol levels due to a particular stage of the production process that involves freezing it and removing a percentage of the water from the beer, making it more "concentrated."

KÖLSCH

FAMILY: TOP FERMENTATION
CATEGORY: LIGHT HYBRID BEER
STYLE: KÖLSCH
ORIGIN: GERMANY (COLOGNE)

This is the quintessential beer of Cologne (in German, "Köln", hence "Kölsch") and one of the few beers with a protected designation of origin. After World War II, the city's producers united to form the Kölsch Konvention, aiming to protect their product. They established simple production guidelines and defined their beer's style. It must be pale and clear (meaning, filtered), top-fermented, hop-flavored, well-rounded with a light body, and most critically, brewed in Cologne.

The Kölsch beers evolved in the 19th century from the brown Altbier. This evolution mirrored how, in England, Pale Ale emerged from Brown Ale, primarily due to the availability of modern light-colored malts born from the scientific and industrial revolutions of that era.

PRODUCTION

Kölsch is crafted with a distinct top-fermenting yeast, but temperatures are kept as low as possible to subtly highlight its fruity profile, a hallmark of this beer. The beer then undergoes cold maturation similar to Lagers, but for a shorter period. Due to this unique process, Kölsch is categorized as a hybrid beer.

It's among Germany's palest beers, featuring a white, albeit short-lived, foam and a subtle aroma of fruit (notably apple) and hops. The flavor is exceptionally well-balanced, ending on a dry note without being overly bitter. A novice might even confuse it with a Pale Lager or a light Golden Ale.

Truly a "session beer," Kölsch is refreshing and consistently enjoyable.

Alcohol volume: Around 4.4-5.2% ABV.
Pairing: Light fare such as chicken salad or the traditional Bratwurst.

BERLINER WEISSE

FAMILY: TOP FERMENTATION
CATEGORY: SOUR ALE
STYLE: BERLINER WEISSE
ORIGIN: GERMANY (BERLIN)

This beer stands out as wholly unique and unconventional. It's a rarity even beyond its native Berlin, where only a handful of small independent brewers, brew-pubs, and a larger conglomerate that owns two renowned labels, produce it. It's among the few beers with a protected designation of origin.

PRODUCTION

In its essence, this beer is multi-dimensional and enigmatically distinct. It undoubtedly qualifies as a Weiss due to its generous wheat malt content, but it lacks the hallmark characteristics of Bavarian Weizen, showcasing only a mild wheat flavor and vivacious carbonation. While it's a top-fermented beer (thanks to the *Saccharomyces cerevisiae* yeast), it's also fortified with a *Lactobacillus* (specifically, the Delbruckii type), which lends the beer its signature acidity and bite, reminiscent of spontaneously fermented Lambic beers. Though it's distinctly tart and exceptionally pale, it's traditionally served diluted with vibrantly colored, sweet fruit syrups like woodruff and raspberry.

CHARACTERISTICS

In its pure form, the beer flaunts a very light straw-yellow hue, occasionally showing opalescent qualities, and topped with a frothy yet fleeting head. The aroma is unmistakably punctuated by mild acidic notes, but the discerning nose might catch subtle fruity and floral undertones.

Crisp, invigorating, and light in both body and alcohol content, its main aim is to quench thirst with its dry finish devoid of any sweetness.

Alcohol content: Typically between 2.8-3.8% ABV.
Pairing: Its acidic sharpness and sophistication, akin to Champagne, position it as an ideal aperitif.

WEIZENBIER (WEISSBIER)

FAMILY: TOP FERMENTATION
CATEGORY: GERMAN WHEAT AND RYE BEER
STYLE: WEIZENBIER (WEISSBIER)
ORIGIN: GERMANY (MUNICH)

This style, among the many crafted by Bavarian brewers, has become widely popular and embraced by the masses. It's distinguished by its significant wheat malt content, never dipping below 50%. The unique character of these beers comes from specific top-fermenting yeasts which, in tandem with the wheat, produce the hallmark spicy clove and ripe banana aroma with phenolic and slightly citric undertones.

However, consumers need to be attentive to the name they encounter on the shelves. "Weiss" (white) points to the color, though in reality, these beers are more pale yellow. On the other hand, "Weizen" (wheat) speaks to its primary ingredient: wheat malt. Apart from these generic names, you might come across variants like "Kristall," indicating a sparkling, filtered, non-refermented beer. "Hefeweizen" (with "Hefe" denoting yeast) is reserved for unfiltered versions that undergo refermentation, resulting in an opalescent and richer hue—these are the most common.

Additionally, there are other Weizen beers outside this style: the Dunkel Weizen, named for their darker hue ("Dunkel" means dark), where the fruity aromas give way to roasted coffee and licorice. Then there's the Weizenbock and the Weizen Doppel-Bock: dark wheat beers that possess the intricate character and higher alcohol content akin to Bocks and Doppel-Bocks.

These beers are refreshingly straightforward and universally appealing. However, they occasionally face unjust disdain from certain "experts", perhaps forgetting that the beer's legacy remained untouched by the renowned Purity Law due to the Bavarian royal family's exclusive production rights.

Many aficionados savor it with an elegantly poised lemon slice on the glass's rim. But as the saying goes, "de gustibus non est disputandum" (in matters of taste, there can be no disputes). Sample both presentations and determine your preference.

Alcohol content: Typically between 4.3-5.6% ABV.
Pairing: In Munich, it's a treat paired with white Vienna sausage and sweet mustard for a mid-morning delight.

GOSE

FAMILY: TOP FERMENTATION (HYBRID)
CATEGORY: CURRENTLY BEING DEFINED
STYLE: GOSE
ORIGIN: GERMANY (GOSLAR AND LEIPZIG)

Today, Gose is associated with Leipzig, the city that championed and rejuvenated it. However, the beer's roots trace back to Goslar, a town nestled along the Gose River. Around the year 1000, Goslar flourished due to newfound silver and copper deposits and its notable beer production. Local brewers utilized water that was notably saline, likely due to the abundant mineral-rich subsoil, giving the beer its distinctive salted profile.

As mining waned in the early Middle Ages, the town's population dwindled, prompting many Gose brewers to seek opportunities elsewhere. Many relocated to Leipzig, where their salted beer found a growing audience. By the early 20th century, Gose had become Leipzig's predominant beer. Its immense popularity even threatened Goslar brewers to the point that Gose production was banned by the local council. Post World War II, within what was then the German Democratic Republic or East Germany, Gose experienced a significant downturn. It wasn't until the late 1980s that a determined beer aficionado, renovating a former Gosen tavern, decided to reintroduce the beverage. This renewed Gose, however, found little interest among nearby brewers, compelling him to collaborate with a Berlin-based brewery. Today, while producers remain few, the enthusiasm Gose incites in those who taste it is undeniable.

PRODUCTION

Gose stands out globally: it incorporates salt, offering a briny taste; it's brewed with a significant amount of wheat malt, classifying it as a Weiss beer; it's seasoned with both coriander and hops, adding a spicy kick; and it's fermented with top-fermenting yeast and lactic bacteria, giving it a sharp, hybrid fermentation profile.

CHARACTERISTICS

Presenting a golden, clear appearance topped by a robust, enduring white foam, Gose possesses a light-to-medium body. Its aroma, though subtle, foretells the beer's spicy and sharp attributes, both of which dominate the palate, complemented by a surprising salty twist that can intrigue but is invariably enjoyed. The beer is refreshing, dry, and thirst-quenching.

Alcohol content: Typically around 4.5-5% ABV.
Pairing: Ideal with seafood.

CZECH REPUBLIC

B consumption in the Czech Republic is nothing short of remarkable. On average, each citizen consumes around 45 US gallons (170 liters) annually. Compare this to the US, where the average is about 18 gallons (70 liters), and it's clear that brewing is deeply embedded in the Czech way of life.

While in regions like Bavaria and Franconia the local pub is often adjoined to the brewery, Bohemia boasts an array of clubs, bars, cafes, and pubs where the first beer is just the beginning. That said, there are breweries where you can enjoy your drink on-site, especially those historic ones that endured the Iron Curtain era. Many of these have since become part of larger conglomerates, like Pilsner Urquell, which is now under the umbrella of South African giant, SAB Miller (also the owner of brands like Peroni and Nastro Azzurro). In the historic district of Pilsen, beer enthusiasts can savor the delightful unfiltered, unpasteurized Pils still brewed nearby.

Traditionally, Czech beers are bottom-fermented. However, the Pils style only made its debut in the mid-19th century. The classic Czech brews vary in color from golden yellow to dark amber, exhibit hints of roasted malts, and generally contain low alcohol levels. Their affordability, coupled with their smooth taste, is perhaps the key to their immense popularity. These beers beckon you to take another sip; each drink enticing the next.

If you find yourself at U Fleků in central Prague, you can sample a beer whose recipe dates back to 1499: a delightful Dunkel (German for "dark") with an alcohol content of 4.6% abv. Though modern brewing methods have likely evolved its taste, the beer remains captivating, especially when enjoyed at the restaurant overlooking a brewery steeped in over five centuries of history.

A word of caution for travelers in Prague and its vicinity: alcohol content isn't always presented as alcohol by volume (e.g., 5% abv). More often than not, you'll see it expressed in degrees Plato. For instance, a beer labeled 13° doesn't indicate a high alcoholic content; it translates to approximately 4.5% abv.

BOHEMIAN PILSNER

FAMILY: BOTTOM FERMENTATION
CATEGORY: PILSNER
STYLE: BOHEMIAN PILSNER
ORIGIN: CZECH REPUBLIC

The Bohemian Pilsner stands as a gold standard for pale hoppy beers. The myriad of names—Pilsen, Pilsener, Pilsner, and Pils—all trace their roots back to the Bohemian city of Plzeň (known as Pilsen in German), the birthplace of this iconic beer. The beer owes its inception to Josef Groll, a forward-thinking German brewer brought over from Bavaria. He integrated newly developed techniques from the industrial revolution - like the use of bottom-fermenting yeast, meticulous control of the malting process, and the advent of thermometers and refrigeration - to craft clear, pale beers. Josef's genius was in fusing his expertise with the exceptional regional ingredients: the aromatic Saaz hops, renowned Moravian malt, and the soft waters of Plzeň.

The outcome? A groundbreaking golden brew that redefined beer, which until then had hues of red-brown or dark. The invention of drinking glasses further enhanced its visual appeal.

However, caution is advised for the discerning drinker. The market, flush with this beer style, offers both exceptional brews and mediocre renditions. Regrettably, the names Pils, Pilsner, or Pilsener are up for grabs since they weren't trademarked originally. Seek out the genuine article bearing the "Urquell" descriptor.

PRODUCTION

Utilizing bottom-fermenting yeast, Pils malts, noble hops, and soft water, the ideal Bohemian Pilsner is traditionally brewed using multiple decoction (though multi-step infusion is the modern approach) and is matured for an extended period in cold conditions.

CHARACTERISTICS

Radiating a pale golden hue, even the handcrafted versions maintain clarity and brightness. Its fine, white foam is abundant and enduring. Its aromatic profile is subtly intricate with herbaceous and floral notes.

Among Lagers, Pilsners are on the bitterer end, yet it's a refined bitterness, never harsh. This bitterness is harmoniously offset by the body and malts, emphasizing balance and synergy over potency or any single standout trait.

Alcohol content: Typically ranges between 4.5-5.4% abv.
Pairing: Perfect with lemon-marinated veal slices, drizzled with oil and served atop fresh arugula.

AUSTRIA

Austria has long held a significant spot in beer's storied history, most notably with its famed "Vienna" malt. Celebrated for its amber hue, gentle flavor, and smoothness, Vienna malt ranks alongside renowned counterparts such as Pilsner, Pale, and Munich malts.

In the mid-1800s, Anton Dreher, a Viennese brewing entrepreneur, pioneered the beer style fondly named after his city. This amber Lager distinguished itself with a unique character, setting it apart from its German counterparts, which also made their mark in Austria. Dreher's creation not only ramped up his production but also found an ardent following in Italy, particularly regions transitioning from the Austrian Empire to the emergent Italian nation.

Historical ties also trace Vienna beers to Mexico, ruled briefly by Habsburg Maximilian I. These beers found a new home in Central America, and while locally adapted, they still resonate with their Austrian roots.

Regrettably, in today's age of brewing homogenization, particularly in Lagers, Vienna-style beers are on the brink of obscurity. Their renaissance owes much to artisanal brewers who, with a commitment to excellence, breathe new life into vanishing styles.

Yet, the allure of Vienna beers endures, especially in cozy Stube, traditional spaces warmed by prominently placed stoves. These beers beautifully complement Austrian culinary delights. Innovations, such as employing hops from the New World and introducing contemporary beer styles, are gaining traction, primarily in local brew-pubs striving to cement their foothold in a competitive market.

Another feather in Austria's brewing cap is the Trappist beer, Gregorius, from Stift Engelszell Abbey. Crafted in silence and adhering to the stringent rules of the Trappist monks, this beer, influenced by Belgian traditions, is potent and defies local brewing norms but remains true to monastic traditions. Since its brewing aligns with Trappist standards, each bottle proudly displays the "Authentic Trappist Product" hexagonal label.

VIENNA LAGER

FAMILY: BOTTOM FERMENTATION
CATEGORY: EUROPEAN AMBER LAGER
STYLE: VIENNA LAGER
ORIGIN: AUSTRIA

The Vienna Lager finds its genesis in the ancient Märzen beers, with its tale intertwined with brewing technological advancements. Two intrepid brewers, Anton Dreher of Vienna and Gabriel Sedlmayr of Munich, endeavored to revolutionize Märzen beers' hue, experimenting with novel lighter, even amber malts termed "Vienna."

While both were pioneers, Dreher took a bolder route, crafting a beer not as pale as Pils but noticeably lighter than traditional Märzen. Borrowing from Sedlmayr's repertoire, Dreher adopted the nascent low-fermentation yeast. Thus, the distinct style of Vienna beers emerged in Austria, while Munich saw the advent of "Viennese-style Märzen." Intriguingly, these Munich beers, later crafted with the novel Munich malt, evolved into what is renowned today as the Oktoberfest, first introduced at Bavaria's iconic beer fest.

CHARACTERISTICS
Vienna Lagers, with their amber-copper hue and enduring white foam, epitomize the malt's opulence and grace in both aroma and taste. Hops make a subtle appearance towards the end, perfectly offsetting the malt's sweetness, ensuring a finish that continually delights.

This sublime beer teeters on the brink of obscurity. Let's champion its preservation, one sip at a time!

Alcohol content: Approximately 4.5-5.5% abv.
Pairing: A sumptuous tomato, mozzarella, and sausage pizza.

UNITED STATES

Since the 1970s, the United States has been instrumental in revitalizing the global fervor for beer, marking the era as "The Modern Renaissance" of brewing. The essence of this revival wasn't corporate but individualistic.

Rather than vast conglomerates dictating tastes and styles, the reins of brewing returned to individual enthusiasts and brewmasters. These passionate pioneers emphasized the personal touch in beer-making, challenging the paradigm of distant, faceless mega-corporations. No longer was beer's character shaped by detached market research or the cold calculations of profit margins. Instead, it was the brewer's heart and skill that breathed life into each bottle and pint.

Starting from humble beginnings, many of these brewers transitioned from homebrewing enthusiasts to full-fledged artisans. Even with modest equipment and limited resources, they endeavored to create unique beers that stood out from the generic offerings of the time. Through sheer determination and a community-focused approach, they began reintroducing the public to the vast spectrum of flavors that beer could offer.

Local breweries became community hubs. They weren't just places to buy beer; they were sites of learning, celebration, and camaraderie. Festivals, workshops, tours, and events sprouted, all aimed at educating the public and fostering a new beer culture. Slogans like "Support your Local Brewery" not only inspired loyalists but also roped in novices to the burgeoning craft beer movement.

Remarkably, these small breweries didn't view each other through the lens of cutthroat competition. Instead, they shared knowledge, collaborated, and jointly procured resources. Their collective vision wasn't just about individual success but about elevating the entire craft beer domain. This unity, combined with the vast U.S. market and a palpable distinction from bland commercial beers, fueled their unprecedented success.

In essence, the U.S. craft beer movement wasn't just a shift in production; it was a renaissance of community, flavor, and authenticity.

The evolution of craft beer in the United States is an intriguing blend of rediscovery and innovation. This industry's meteoric rise is largely credited to its ability to listen and cater to the evolving tastes of consumers. Craft beer enthusiasts yearned for more than just beer; they sought a multi-dimensional experience that teased their palates, emotions, and curiosities.

In the formative years, American brewers turned to the time-honored brewing traditions of Europe. These European styles provided a foundation upon which brewers could innovate and experiment. The mere reintroduction of European brews was, in many ways, a radical shift in a domestic market dominated by mass-produced, one-note lagers. Yet, it was merely the beginning.

As the craft beer movement picked up steam, brewers began to infuse these European styles with distinct American flair, giving birth to variants like the American IPA, American Barley Wine, and American Lager.

The descriptor "American" was not just about geography; it was a testament to the creativity and ingenuity behind these brews.

Hops became the cornerstone of the American craft beer revolution. The rediscovery and incorporation of diverse hop varieties allowed brewers to produce beers with aromatic profiles previously unknown in the beer world. From the tantalizing citrus notes of grapefruit and mandarin to the woody, resinous aromas reminiscent of pine, hops transformed the olfactory and gustatory experience of beer drinking.

The audacity of American brewers didn't stop at experimenting with flavors. They pushed the boundaries of bitterness, challenging and expanding the palate of their consumers. Like the acquired taste for unsweetened espresso, the love for hop-forward, bitter brews is an evolved preference, deviating from the instinctual human gravitation towards sweet flavors.

Such flavor-forward audacity raises an interesting hypothetical: How would the trajectory of craft beer change if regulatory systems began taxing beers based on bitterness rather than alcohol content? While this remains a speculative thought experiment, it underscores the delicate interplay between culture, market demands, and regulation.

The American craft beer movement's journey is far from over. As it evolves, one thing remains clear: the relentless pursuit of quality, innovation, and a desire to offer drinkers an immersive experience will always define craft beer. And as for what the future holds? Only time (and perhaps the next pint) will tell.

AMERICAN PALE ALE (APA)

FAMILY: TOP FERMENTATION
CATEGORY: AMERICAN ALE
STYLE: AMERICAN PALE ALE (APA)
ORIGIN: UNITED STATES

American Pale Ales, commonly known as APA, are an American adaptation of the English Pale Ales using local ingredients. The hops, originally from Europe and transplanted to America before being crossbred with new selections, significantly influenced first the world of American brewing and then the rest of the world. APA beers marked a historic departure from tradition with their low alcohol content, new aromas, fresh flavors, and subtle bitterness. They ignited a revolution that's still in motion, leading to the emergence of many new beer styles such as the American IPA, Double IPA, Imperial IPA, and numerous reinterpretations appearing globally.

PRODUCTION

Top-fermentation is employed. The primary ingredients are American-produced Pale malt, a touch of malt for sweetness, occasionally Roasted, and, most importantly, hops—especially those that emit citrus fragrances. Hops are added predominantly during late-hopping (in the final stages of boiling the wort) and often in dry-hopping (during the beer's maturation phase) to accentuate the aromatic characteristics of this style.

CHARACTERISTICS

The color can range considerably, from a cloudy amber to a deep amber, depending on the malts used. In contrast, the foam is white, creamy, and long-lasting. The fragrances of American hops overshadow the malts, offering citrus, resinous, and herbaceous notes. The body is light with a moderate carbonation level. If the hopping is too aggressive, one might detect an undesirable astringency. The sweet, roasted or toasted flavors of the malts are offset by the bitterness, achieving a harmonious balance. The citrus and resinous tones of the hops persist in the extended aftertaste.

Alcohol content: 4.5-6.2% abv.
Pairing: These are refreshing beers suitable for any time of day and are perfect as an aperitif due to their low alcohol content and invigorating nature.

STANDARD AMERICAN LAGER

FAMILY: BOTTOM FERMENTATION
CATEGORY: LIGHT LAGER
STYLE: STANDARD AMERICAN LAGER
ORIGIN: UNITED STATES

This is essentially an international style encompassing the typical Pale Lagers widely available in the mass market. Due to its use of large quantities of cereals, such as corn and rice—ingredients historically employed in American beer-making—it is categorized under the United States section.

Commonly, the economical grains, corn and rice, aren't combined, but in some cheaper beers, both may be present, sometimes joined by another cost-effective addition: sugar. Laws, which differ from one country to the next, have established constraints on these additives, which otherwise could reach significant proportions.

The "craft beer" movement neither sought to refine nor elevate the Lager style, nor did it possess the means to. This may have been a deliberate decision, motivated by a desire to distinctly differentiate from mass-market offerings by creating an entirely unique brew. However, Lagers, with their extended cold maturation phase, have a longer production cycle. This requires more storage tanks, increased financial commitment, and larger storage spaces, which might be prohibitive for many small-scale breweries.

CHARACTERISTICS

These beers are exceptionally pale, featuring fleeting white foam and subtle aromas of malt, corn, and hops. They offer a refreshing palate, have a light body, and conclude with a dry, brief finish due to the pronounced carbonation that tingles the tongue.

It's the kind of beer best enjoyed chilled, even straight from the bottle, without overanalyzing its nuances.

Alcohol content: Approximately 4.2-5.3% abv.
Pairing: Its mild character doesn't necessarily complement gourmet dishes, but it pairs perfectly with a classic hot dog.

IMPERIAL IPA

FAMILY: TOP FERMENTATION
CATEGORY: INDIA PALE ALE (IPA)
STYLE: IMPERIAL IPA
ORIGIN: UNITED STATES

The Imperial IPA is a style that has emerged more recently, aiming to categorize the more robust versions of American IPAs that bear labels adorned with descriptors like "double," "extra," or "extreme" IPA. The American brewers' ambition to innovate and then intensify led them primarily to hops, deploying them in astonishing amounts at every possible step of the brewing process. In certain instances, specialized equipment was devised solely to optimize the aromatic potential of hops. Presently, brewers from other countries are drawing inspiration from the Imperial IPA's liberal use of hops.

PRODUCTION

Malts are pivotal in counterbalancing the hops' bitterness. These malts, whether American, English, or German, are introduced at various stages: from mashing, through the whirlpool phase, and during maturation, in a multifaceted blend reminiscent of alchemical practices. The top-fermenting yeast is typically neutral, not anticipated to yield esters, but rather to focus on alcohol generation through attenuation.

CHARACTERISTICS

Coloration varies from a rich gold to copper, accompanied by a fine-grained and enduring foam.

Aromatic hops reign supreme, melding into a multifaceted bouquet encompassing citrus, floral, fruity, herbal, and resinous scents.

The malt's sweetness offsets the pronounced bitterness, providing a semblance of balance to the beer, which still retains an enduring, evident bitterness. The beer has a medium body, moderate to high carbonation, and its modest dryness bolsters its drinkability, leaving behind a subtle alcoholic warmth. The finish is prolonged and robust, with predominant citrusy bitter undertones. In some instances, it can be regarded as a contemplative beer with soothing balsamic hints.

Alcohol content: Ranges from 7.5 to 10% abv.

AMERICAN IPA

FAMILY: TOP FERMENTATION
CATEGORY: INDIA PALE ALE (IPA)
STYLE: AMERICAN IPA
ORIGIN: UNITED STATES

American India Pale Ales represent the U.S. micro-breweries' take on the classic English IPA. Their divergence from traditional India Pale Ales stems from the use of local ingredients and, notably, the brewers' generous use of hops, predominantly from the north-west coast, aiming for novel flavors and enhanced bitterness. While many opt for hop varieties known as the 4 Cs (Cascade, Columbus, Centennial, Chinook), others like Amarillo, Willamette, and more recently, Citra and Simcoe, have gained popularity, especially along the West Coast of California, where the modern "hop rush" mirrors the historic gold rush. These IPAs are essentially stronger and hoppier versions of American Pale Ales.

PRODUCTION

Pale malts form the primary grain blend, supplemented by Caramel malts and occasionally roasted hops. Hops, in significant quantities, are integrated throughout the mashing process to amplify both bitterness and aroma. Dry-hopping, a technique involving generous hop addition to boost beer aroma, is a common practice. The chosen yeasts are typically neutral, ensuring they don't produce esters but contribute to the beer's attenuation (dryness).

CHARACTERISTICS

The beer's hue spans from golden to a cloudy amber, occasionally boasting orange tints, and is generally clear. Its white, fine-grained foam is enduring.

An immediate burst of intense hop aroma greets the drinker, showcasing lemony, resinous, floral, and fruity notes, overshadowing the subtle undertones of Caramel malts. Smooth on the palate, its body ranges from medium to light with moderate to high carbonation. While hops take center stage in flavor, the malt, with its caramel (and occasionally roasted) notes, balances the palpable yet manageable bitterness. The lingering aftertaste is a hoppy explosion, consistent with the initial aroma.

Alcohol content: 5.5-7.5% abv.
Pairing: They are an excellent match for barbecues, complementing grilled meats and sausages.

CASCADIAN DARK ALE

FAMILY: TOP FERMENTATION
CATEGORY: INDIA PALE ALE (IPA)
STYLE: CASCADIAN DARK ALE OR BLACK IPA
ORIGIN: UNNITED STATES

Cascadian Dark Ales stand as a shining testament to American brewing innovation. Now an officially acknowledged style, this beer manages to capture the essence of a Stout's darkness paired with the hoppiness of an IPA.

Originating in the Pacific Northwest of the U.S., specifically between the Cascade Range and the Yakima and Willamette valleys, this region is agriculturally rich, producing barley for beer and, notably, serving as the primary growing region for American hops. Consequently, it's a pivotal hub for the creation of many modern aromatic hops, vital to the Cascadian Dark Ale style.

Initially, local brewers introduced darker versions of their hop-forward beers at festivals and special events. Rapidly gaining favor among enthusiasts, these beers soon became a staple offering for many. Recognizing this emerging trend, brewers elsewhere were quick to join the fray, prompting the need for a distinct style classification. Some, wishing to sidestep regional nomenclature, opted for the term "Black IPA."

CHARACTERISTICS

At first glance, the Cascadian Dark Ale's defining characteristic is its rich hue, spanning from deep brown to inky black. Yet, contrary to appearances, it doesn't have the powerful roasted malt aromas and flavors one might expect. The dark malts used are stripped of their inherent bitterness or are naturally colored malt extracts. Blind taste-testers might be hard-pressed to identify its malt presence, as its primary contribution is color.

Moreover, this beer boasts a robust hoppy personality typical of an IPA. Dominated by the regional hops' lemony, spicy, resinous, and floral profiles (think Cascade, Amarillo, Simcoe, Columbus, Centennial, and Chinook), these flavors and scents take center stage. Expect a decidedly dry and bitter finish with a medium-light body. Brewers typically use "neutral" yeasts to prevent ester production, further accentuating the hop aroma.

One unexpected pleasure of these beers is the synergy between dark malts and certain hops, eliciting minty and rosemary-like aromas.

Alcohol content: Approximately 6-8% abv.
Pairing: Best enjoyed with raw fish and sushi.

AMERICAN BARLEY WINE

FAMILY: TOP FERMENTATION
CATEGORY: STRONG ALE
STYLE: AMERICAN BARLEY WINE
ORIGIN: UNITED STATES

While the English Barley Wine provided foundational inspiration, the American version crafted by micro-breweries distinguishes itself through its pronounced hop presence. The bitterness in the American variety is striking, yet it harmoniously melds with elegant aromas laden with citrus and balsamic nuances. Moving away from the restraint of English versions, the American Barley Wine encapsulates contemporary brewers' penchant for pushing boundaries, continually vying to create the boldest, richest, and most opulent brew.

CHARACTERISTICS

Visually, American Barley Wine boasts an intense amber-red hue, seldom venturing into brown territory. Its foam is fine, with its amount and persistence varying across samples.

The aroma is an intoxicating medley born from generous malt and hop contributions, supplemented by ethyl notes and fruity esters emerging from fermentation.

On the palate, it unfurls with a richness and fullness that are emblematic of its character. In these brews, sweetness and bitterness run side by side, harmoniously linked by the alcohol. Yet, as the tasting progresses, hops boldly forge ahead, leaving a lasting impression on the finish.

Conducting a vertical tasting—comparing freshly brewed to aged variants—provides fascinating insights into its maturation potential. While some might dismiss these beers as overindulgent experiments, the finest examples can evoke unparalleled sensory delights.

Alcohol content: Ranges from 8-13% abv.
Pairing: Typically relished as a post-meal indulgence, certain aromatic versions of Barley Wine also intriguingly complement intricate desserts.

ITALY

The Italian peninsula has a rich brewing tradition. In the past, most cities had one or more breweries that produced cold beers intended for consumption during the hotter months. These beers were viewed as summer drinks, akin to wine, but were also enjoyed with meals and in taverns, even during the winter months and between meals. However, as the 20th century progressed, a slow decline set in, leading to the closure of most breweries, leaving behind few memories of the beers they once produced. Some breweries were acquired by large industrial groups, with a few retaining the original brand names (such as Peroni Nastro Azzurro, Moretti, Ichnusa, and Angelo Poretti), while others eliminated all traces of the former brand. Notably, Forst acquired Menabrea of Biella in Piedmont, allowing it considerable autonomy.

By the early 1990s, the situation had become quite distressing. Only the industrial breweries remained active, local breweries were virtually nonexistent, and beer consumption was on the decline. A handful of pubs offered imported beers that were somewhat unique and interesting compared to the bland industrial lagers. However, by the late 1990s, a shift occurred as small, and often microscopic, craft breweries began to emerge. This marked the beginning of the Italian Renaissance in brewing. The movement started with a few pioneers and grew exponentially, with estimates now suggesting there are over 600 breweries in the country.

Interestingly, in Italy, beer is still predominantly seen as a refreshing drink to be consumed between meals, lacking the cultural significance enjoyed by wine. Paradoxically, Italian brewers have found the most success in other countries, particularly in the United States. In just 18 years, Italy has gained a prominent position and reputation in the world of traditional brewing, revitalizing the art.

Italian brewers initially followed brewing traditions from Anglo-Saxon, German, and Belgian styles before incorporating North American influences. Some beers were inspired by German styles like Kölsch, Pils, or Keller, reinvented by Italian brewers. Italy also introduced innovative beer styles using local ingredients like chestnuts, which were incorporated in various forms, such as raw, boiled, minced, roasted, or as flour.

Many breweries have started to create beers closely tied to their specific regions. Due to the challenge of growing hops in Italy, which is time-consuming and costly, native hops are rarely used. Instead, local cereals, barley malt, and indigenous spices and fruits grown near the breweries are commonly featured.

Furthermore, numerous pubs, either newly opened or converted, are now offering Italian-made beers, while some restaurants are expanding their beverage offerings by including a beer list alongside their wine selections. Beer has transformed from being wine's lesser counterpart to a product of equal dignity, even making its way into highly regarded Michelin-starred restaurants.

Italian brewers have also begun to draw inspiration from the world of wine. Italy's strong wine culture has influenced brewers who adapt to their local environment. Many breweries are located in wine regions or have close ties to winemakers, resulting in beers that bridge the gap between brewing and winemaking. These beers may utilize grapes directly, grape juice, wort, cooked grape wort, or even grape marc to achieve desired flavors. Some brewers employ traditional Champagne methods, including riddling, disgorgement, and liqueur d'expédition (a sugar solution in wine) to produce these unique creations. Each of these beers not only reflects the character of the grapes but also evolves over time due to the interaction of natural yeast from the wort or grape skins with the selected beer yeast.

Italy's contribution to the world of spontaneous fermentation and barrel-aged beers is significant, resulting in contemporary and innovative beer styles that coexist with tradition. While there may not be an official style designation, Italy is making numerous contributions to the ever-evolving world of brewing.

CHESTNUT BEER

FAMILY: ALTA E BOTTOM FERMENTATION
CATEGORY: FRUIT BEER
STYLE: CHESTNUT BEER
ORIGIN: ITALY

The use of chestnuts in beer has become a defining characteristic of the emerging Italian brewing tradition. Chestnut trees are widespread throughout Italy, with hardly a valley, mountain, or hill lacking their presence. These versatile nuts are frequently incorporated into local cuisine, featured in both savory and sweet dishes, from main courses to chestnut-based desserts like marrons glacés and roasted chestnuts. Brewers have recognized the value of chestnuts as a connection to the local terroir, although blending malts, yeasts, and chestnuts is a complex task. Consequently, there is no official style designation, as each brewer strives to create a unique chestnut beer. The "Chestnut beer, top and bottom-fermenting" category in the Italian Beer of the Year competition, organized by the Unionbirrai, acknowledges the growing prominence of chestnut beers.

PRODUCTION

Chestnuts are employed in various forms—raw, boiled, minced, or as flour—based on the brewer's chosen recipe. Some brewers also incorporate pure chestnut honey into their beers, but in such cases, the beer is often more appropriately described as honey beer rather than chestnut beer. Brewers have the liberty to select malts, hops (although hops are not typically a dominant feature), and yeast types, whether top or bottom fermenting.

CHARACTERISTICS

The appearance of chestnut beers varies according to the chosen malts, as do the bouquet and flavors. In all instances, chestnut flavors take center stage, with notes of raw chestnuts, roasted chestnuts, and marrons glacés prominently featured. These chestnut flavors are never overshadowed by the malts, even if the malts are toasted or roasted, nor by the hops.

Alcohol content: Varies.
Pairing: Chestnut beers are versatile in their pairings, as they complement any dish incorporating chestnuts, from turkey with chestnut stuffing to roasted chestnuts.

ITALIAN LAGER

FAMILY: BOTTOM FERMENTATION
CATEGORY: PALE LAGER
STYLE: ITALIAN LAGER (style not yet codified and in course of definition)
ORIGIN: ITALY

The world of Italian lager is one of burgeoning creativity, where small independent brewers are charting a path toward the development of unique beer styles. Unlike regions with well-established brewing traditions, Italian lagers have not yet concretely defined their own precise style. However, this lack of rigid structure has allowed local brewers to explore and innovate, leading to the emergence of several highly appreciated beer types within Italy and beyond.

Among these innovative styles are Pale Lagers. While large national breweries in Italy and elsewhere continue to produce pale lagers with relatively traditional and bland profiles, independent brewers are pushing the boundaries. These craft brewers are crafting pale, bottom-fermenting beers with distinctive characteristics that set them apart. These beers typically have a slightly higher alcohol content compared to similar styles, featuring a greater concentration of bitter, resinous, and aromatic hop notes, encompassing floral, spicy, and fruity aromas. Hops are generously used, often employing dry-hopping techniques, and fermentation temperatures are sometimes elevated beyond the usual range for bottom fermentation. These unique brewing approaches aim to emphasize both the olfactory and gustatory sensations of the beer.

The annual competition for the best Italian artisanal beers, Beer of the Year, has recognized the significance of this particular beer style with a dedicated category.

In the broader international beer landscape, some may view this as a departure from traditional styles, but it exemplifies the essence of innovation in brewing. History has shown that countless beer styles have been invented, modified, disappeared, and occasionally revived over time. Only time will reveal the ultimate fate of this burgeoning Italian trend, still in its early stages but brimming with dynamism and potential.

DENMARK AND NORWAY

Denmark and Norway, though distinct countries, serve as a prime example of the modernization of brewing, and their brewing scenes have undergone significant transformations in recent years.

Historically, the Danish brewing landscape was dominated by Carlsberg, founded in 1847 by Jacob Christian Jacobsen. Carlsberg's influence extended worldwide, and it played a pivotal role in brewing history. Notably, Emil Christian Hansen isolated *Saccharomyces carlsbergensis*, a bottom-fermenting yeast strain that became a foundation for lager production worldwide.

In contemporary Denmark, a wave of brewing innovation has surged, largely propelled by Mikkel Borg Bjergsø, known as one of the foremost "gypsy brewers." Bjergsø founded the Mikkeller brand, which has disrupted Danish brewing traditions with its unconventional approach. Other brewers, with or without their own breweries, such as Amager, Beer Here, and Mikkel's twin brother Jeppe with Evil Twin (now based in Brooklyn, USA), have invigorated the Danish beer scene. They have boldly experimented with hops from around the world, diverse grains, and wood maturation techniques. Effective marketing has been crucial, especially for brewers without their own facilities, helping them carve out a niche in the market for innovative beers.

In neighboring Norway, where industrial lagers had dominated for over a century, traditional brewing experienced a revival in 1989 with the establishment

of Oslo Mikrobryggeri, a brewpub that paved the way for subsequent openings. Norwegian brewers are particularly inspired by American innovations. Notably, Mike Murphy, a brewer from Philadelphia, left his mark on the Italian and Danish brewing scenes before relocating to Stavanger, Norway, where he became the master brewer of Lervig Aktiebryggeri.

Brewers like Haandbryggeriet in Drammen and Nøgne Ø in Grimstad also contribute to the vibrant local brewing scene. They collaborate with other brewers, participate in global events and fairs, and export a significant portion of their premium products, helping Norwegian brewing innovations gain international recognition. Microbreweries have disrupted the local market accustomed to conventional production with their aromatic and flavorful beers. In under a decade, Nøgne Ø has produced over 100 different beers, while HaandBryggeriet has created more than 70.

The northern Norwegian climate is not conducive to hop cultivation, so brewers rely on imports, particularly from North America and Australasia. They blend these hops with locally sourced ingredients like cereals (such as rye) and indigenous berries and fruits for special brews. The Norwegians' interpretation of Anglo-American-inspired IPAs, particularly those incorporating rye malt, sets them apart. Additionally, the use of barrels for aging beer has become a customary practice in microbreweries.

BALTIC PORTER

FAMILY: BOTTOM FERMENTATION
(but some examples use top fermentation)
CATEGORY: PORTER
STYLE: BALTIC PORTER
ORIGIN: BALTIC SEA COUNTRIES

Baltic Porters are dark beers that fall somewhere between the robust Porter and the Russian Imperial Stout in terms of style. Their origins can be traced back to the 19th-century trade of English Porter beers, which were highly popular in the countries around the Baltic Sea and Russia. These historical brews laid the foundation for today's Baltic Porter, which closely resembles the Porters of the past. Baltic Porters are characterized by their increased strength, structure, and intensity when compared to today's English Brown Porters.

PRODUCTION

The key distinction lies in the fact that Baltic Porters are primarily produced in the Baltic region, not in England. They are brewed using bottom-fermenting yeast, which makes them lagers rather than ales (though there are a few top-fermenting examples where fermentation temperatures are kept very low). To prevent dominant toasted and burnt notes, modern dark malts with their bitterness removed (similar to the approach used for Schwarzbier) are used. Additionally, large quantities of Munich and Vienna malts, along with some Crystal malts, are included in the brewing process.

CHARACTERISTICS

Baltic Porters exhibit a color ranging from very dark copper to brown, but they should not be pitch black. They boast a thick, long-lasting foam with a cappuccino-like hue. While they lack the strong roasted coffee aroma commonly found in Russian Imperial Stouts, they do feature intense malty notes reminiscent of English Brown Porters. You'll also detect fruity esters, such as raisins, black cherries, and blackcurrants, along with subtle alcoholic notes. These beers typically start sweetish but are balanced by the emergence of dark malts, leading to a smooth finish enriched by hints of coffee and licorice. The high carbonation helps lighten their full, generous body. Baltic Porters are complex yet approachable beers.

Alcohol content: Approximately 5.5-9.5% ABV.
Pairing: Baltic Porters pair excellently with roast meats and smoked dishes.

RYE IPA

FAMILY: TOP FERMENTATION
CATEGORY: NOT YET DEFINED
STYLE: RYE IPA (BUT NOT YET DEFINED)
ORIGIN: UNITED STATES

This style, not yet officially recognized, is based on IPAs featuring a rather unusual ingredient: rye. This rugged grain, less renowned than barley, finds widespread use worldwide in crafting specialties like rye bread, rye whisky, and traditional rye beers such as the Roggenbier in Bavaria, and the distinctly unique Finnish Sahti. However, it should not be mistaken for the relatively recent Rye IPA, sometimes referred to as Rye PA for ease of pronunciation.

These beers have garnered significant acclaim, initially limited to the United States. The trend kicked off when the Bear Republic micro-brewery produced "Hop Rod Rye," an Imperial IPA rich in rye malt, which went on to claim several awards in official competitions during the early 2000s.

Before long, pioneering brewers in Scandinavia embarked on successful experiments with this beer style, leading us to include it in the chapter dedicated to Denmark and Norway. Rye IPAs amplify the characteristics of the American IPA, further enriched by the complex, spicy, peppery, and earthy profile of rye, which imparts a delightful dryness to the finish.

Alcohol content: approximately 6-8% ABV.

SMOKED BEERS AND BEERS MATURED IN WOOD

Legend has it that during one of the fires at Bamberg Cathedral, the malt warehouse in the adjacent brewery became filled with smoke. The brewer, undeterred, used the smoky malt to make his usual Märzen beer. To everyone's surprise, the beer had a distinct smoky flavor, but fortunately, customers loved it. This marks the birth of Bamberg Rauchbiers. While the veracity of this story is debatable, the smoky beers of Franconia endure, as does the cathedral, which was eventually rebuilt.

These beers exhibit a wide range of characteristics. They typically vary in color from golden to brown, possess a medium body, medium-high carbonation, and an alcohol content that falls between 4.8% and 6%. The degree of smokiness depends on the amount of "rauch" (smoky) malt in the grist, which can range from 20% to 100%. The smoky notes may be accompanied by hints of caramel, toast, and even some herbal hop notes, or alternatively, they may dominate the flavor profile. However, one constant is the yeast: all Franconian beers are bottom-fermented.

In reality, as you explore Franconia, you'll encounter numerous beers that deviate slightly from these parameters. Some may have lower or higher smoky notes, while others exhibit different body profiles, ranging from thin to full-bodied. Essentially, the Purity Law takes a back seat in this part of Franconia, where each brewer follows their own path, starting with a bottom-fermented beer (such as Bock, Hefe-Weizen, Dunkel, Schwarz, Doppelbock, or Hell) and then transforming it into a smoky beer.

Not too far from the German border in eastern Prussia, you'll find Grodziskie or Grätzer beers, exclusively produced with oak-smoked wheat malt. In the city of Grodzisk (known as Grätz in German), the last brewery making this unique beer was acquired and subsequently closed by another brewer within the Heineken Group. Considered a historic beer and almost extinct, it has been revived by enthusiasts who conducted archaeological beer research and managed to recover cells of the original yeast. They successfully resurrected this distinct smoked beer

Smoked and peaty beers must exhibit smoky aromas in both the bouquet and taste, but they can come in any color: clear, amber, or dark.

style in Holland and Germany. Today, you can even find examples of Grätzer beers in the United States. Originally, there were two types: one with higher alcohol content, which later gave way to a lower-alcohol version due to changes in tax regulations.

In the rest of the world, inspired by German tradition and driven by their own creativity, brewers are producing smoked beers. These beers are based on existing beer styles, such as Porter, Robust Porter, and others, to which smoked malt is added. The smoking process often involves using locally available wood or, in some cases, even peat. This broad category also includes German examples that incorporate smoked malt into various beer styles like Pils, Weizenbock, and more. There are no specific constraints regarding alcohol content, color, body, or carbonation levels; the defining characteristic is the use of smoked malt, which imparts both aroma and flavor.

While there's a wide range of smoked beers, an even broader category is beers matured in wooden barrels. Wood, which was historically used for aging beers, was largely replaced by stainless steel in modern brewing, except for some Belgian breweries, especially those practicing spontaneous fermentation. However, many brewers have returned to using barrels to impart unique characters to their beers. These barrels can be from various sources, including port, sherry, red wine, white wine, rum, Scotch whisky, Irish whiskey, Bourbon whiskey, and more. The barrels can introduce flavors like vanilla, toasted bread, caramel, almonds, cocoa, and coffee. Additionally, they can alter the beer's body and dryness. Some barrel-aged beers may also exhibit slight acidity, often due to lactic and acetic notes or the influence of wild yeasts. The specific characteristics of barrel-aged beers depend on the brewer's choices, the length of aging, the type of wood used, and the unpredictable elements of nature.

The United States is a major player in barrel-aging beer, thanks to the size of its cellars and the availability of barrels in the market. Italy also has a growing presence in this area, often repurposing barrels from nearby wineries known to the brewers. Some breweries even experiment with barrels used for balsamic vinegar, vin santo, grappa, and various spirits.

Some beers matured in wooden barrels may develop a high level of effervescence due to the action of microorganisms like Brettanomyces.

THE MAJOR COUNTRIES AND THE MAJOR STYLES OF BEER

HOMEMADE
BEER

FAMILY: YOURS
CATEGORY: WHATEVER YOU LIKE!
STYLE: YOUR PREFERENCE
ORIGIN: YOUR HOME

Home-brewing is not only possible, but it's also a delightful endeavor!

With just a few pieces of simple equipment, some knowledge of the production process, and a strong desire to try home-brewing, you can create beer of any style right in the comfort of your home. As with all things, practice and dedication are essential to achieve the best results. However, there's no denying the satisfaction of sipping on beer you've crafted yourself or sharing it with friends, even if it's not perfect.

You can start with the fermentation of straightforward preparations of already-hopped malt extract. These preparations essentially concentrate the efforts of other brewers who have already prepared a regular barley malt wort, complete with hops for bitterness. By boiling off the water, they create a concentrated extract. As a novice home-brewer, all you need to do is add water, dissolve the contents, and then initiate fermentation by introducing specially prepared yeast. From that point onward, it's the yeast that takes over, doing the work of beer production.

Alternatively, for those who prefer not to use concentrates, there's the all-grain production method. This method involves starting with cereal grains that must be milled, mashed, filtered, boiled, hopped, and finally, fermented. While this approach mirrors the traditional methods used by professional brewers, it demands more time, effort, and space. However, it grants you complete control over every detail of the brewing process.

Today, many websites in various countries sell products for home-brewing, often supplying professional micro-breweries as well. These sources offer high-quality raw materials, basic and advanced equipment, as well as manuals and books on home-brewing techniques—everything you might need and more.

Additionally, there are several national associations and movements of home-brewers and beer enthusiasts. They organize meetings, seminars, guided tastings, training programs, and even competitions where home-brewers can put their creations to the test. However, it's essential to understand that the transition from home-brewing to becoming a professional brewer is not a small step—just as knowing how to cook doesn't automatically make someone a great chef!

24 RECIPES

BY CHEF GIOVANNI RUGGIERI

PAIRING

BEER AND FOOD

When pairing a dish with a particular beer, it's essential to have a good understanding of both elements. The goal is to create a harmonious balance of flavors in the mouth, which can be achieved through either contrast (such as pairing sweetness with bitterness) or similarity (matching bitterness with bitterness or sweetness with sweetness).

One crucial consideration is that the gap between the two elements should not be too wide. For instance, serving an extremely bitter beer with a very sweet dish is not ideal, as bridging the distance between these extremes can be challenging.

Conversely, offering an overly sweet beer with a very sweet dish can be overly cloying. While a sweet beer can complement a sweet dish to some extent and even reduce the overall sensation of sweetness when perfectly balanced, it's important not to overdo it.

The golden rule is that dishes with delicate flavors pair best with simple beers, while dishes with strong and pronounced flavors benefit from more complex and intense beers.

In addition to sweetness and bitterness, consider other beer characteristics like alcohol content, carbonation level, toasting degree, acidity, astringency, and aromatic properties.

Rather than delving deep into the theory, here are some simple yet essential guidelines to encourage experimentation without undue worry. Remember, practice is the best way to learn, and sometimes the most significant discoveries happen by chance. You can relax knowing that an unsuccessful food and beer pairing won't pose a health risk and won't ruin a good beer or dish. If you find that a pairing doesn't work after the first sip and bite, you can always enjoy them separately!

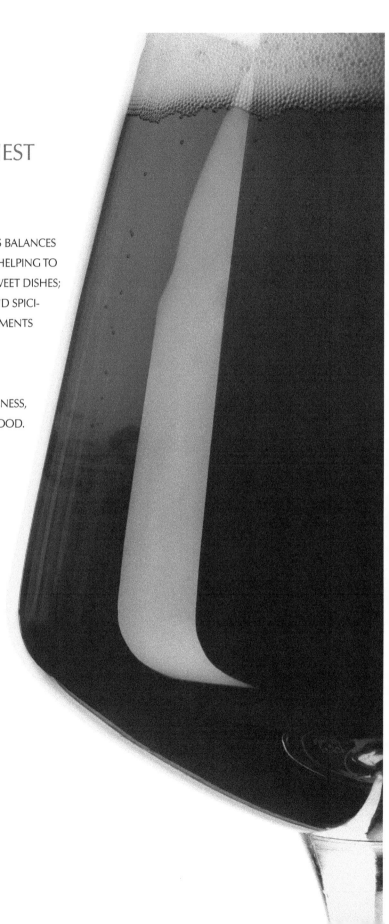

THE COMMONEST PAIRINGS

THE BITTERNESS OF THE HOPS BALANCES THE RICHNESS OF FOOD (BY HELPING TO CLEANSE THE PALATE) AND SWEET DISHES; IT EMPHASIZES PIQUANCY AND SPICINESS IN GENERAL; IT COMPLEMENTS BITTER FLAVORS.

THE SWEETNESS OF THE BEER CONTRASTS WITH THE BITTERNESS, ACIDITY, AND SPICINESS OF FOOD.

ACIDITY BALANCES THE RICHNESS AND FATTINESS OF DISHES.

TOASTED MALT BALANCES SMOKINESS AND CONTRASTS WITH SWEETNESS.

ALCOHOL CONTRASTS WITH FATTY FOODS AND ENHANCES SPICINESS

PIEDMONTESE BEEF
SASHIMI FASSONA BEEF WITH TURNIP
SPROUTS AND PORTER BEER CREAM

SERVES 4

11 1/2 OUNCES (330 G) PIECES OF FASSONA BEEF, TRIMMED
1 1/4 CUPS (300 ML) PORTER BEER
1/3 OUNCES (8 G) SHEET GELATIN
1 PACKET OF SPARKLE DUSTING POWDER
1 SMALL BOWL OF TURNIP SPROUTS
EXTRA-VIRGIN OLIVE OIL
SALT
WHITE WINE VINEGAR

PREPARATION

For the cream, place the sheet gelatin in cold water with a few ice cubes for 10 minutes. Transfer it to a saucepan and warm it over low heat for 1 minute while stirring with a whisk until it is completely dissolved. Gradually add a little beer to the dissolved gelatin while it is still over very low heat, then incorporate the rest of the beer and refrigerate for 12 hours. The following day, blend it in a kitchen mixer until it becomes creamy and frothy. Allow it to rest in the refrigerator.

To prepare the meat, remove any excess fat. Slice it into 1/8-inch (3 mm) thick pieces, arrange them in a steel dish, and season them with a bit of oil and salt.

For the sprouts, trim off the end parts using scissors, then soak them in a bowl of cold water for a few minutes. Drain and season with oil, salt, and white wine vinegar to taste.

Assemble the dish, starting with a layer of the cream at the bottom. Lightly sprinkle the slices of Fassona beef with the sparkle dusting powder using your fingers, and then add the turnip sprouts, seasoned lightly to preserve their pungency.

FRIED COD IN BATTER
WITH BITTER ALE VINAIGRETTE
AND WILD LEAF SALAD

SERVES 4

14 OUNCES (400 G) FRESH COD (GABILO)
1 CUP (150 G) RICE FLOUR
SCANT 1/2 CUP (50 G) TYPE 0 OR ALL-PURPOSE FLOUR
2 CUPS (500 ML) SPARKLING WATER, REFRIGERATED
1/3 CUP+2 TABLESPOONS (100 ML) BITTER ALE
3/4 CUP+2 TABLESPOONS (200 ML) EXTRA-VIRGIN OLIVE OIL
1/2 OUNCES (15 G) BREWER'S YEAST
9 OUNCES (250 G) WILD LEAF SALAD (SMALL RED AND GREEN LEAVES)
PEANUT OIL AS NEEDED
SALT AND PEPPER

PREPARATION

For the vinaigrette, mix the olive oil with the Bitter Ale and salt. Blend with a hand blender until it emulsifies.

For the cod, remove the central spine and cut the fish into pieces about 2 1/2 inches (6 cm) square. For the batter, combine the rice flour and all-purpose flour. Dissolve the yeast in a small amount of the water. Add the remaining chilled sparkling water from the refrigerator, which should be just opened. Mix the batter by hand until it forms a thick, creamy mixture. Test it by dipping a piece of cod into it, making sure it doesn't drip off immediately. Fry until the batter is crisp, but be careful not to let it get brown—it should remain white.

To plate, place the wild leaf salad mixed with the vinaigrette on the bottom of the plate, and then add the pieces of cod that have just been fried in batter.

PORK FILLET COOKED IN BAVARIAN WEIZEN BEER, BARLEY, CABBAGE AND CUMIN

SERVES 4

1 PORK FILLET
1 1/4 CUPS (300 ML) BAVARIAN WEIZEN BEER
1 TABLESPOON (3 G) CUMIN
11 1/2 OUNCES (330 G) CABBAGE
3 1/2 OUNCES (100 G) BARLEY
EXTRA-VIRGIN OLIVE OIL
WHITE WINE VINEGAR
SALT AND PEPPER

PREPARATION

For the pork, heat the beer in a pan to 150°F (65°C). Meanwhile, remove any fatty parts from the pork fillet, season it with salt and pepper, and rub it with oil, massaging it well so that the oil is absorbed. Fry the pork fillet in a very hot non-stick pan. Immerse the meat in the hot beer and cook at a constant temperature for 50 minutes. Remove the fillet from the beer, place it on a dish, and let it cool in the refrigerator.

For the barley, boil salted water and cook the barley in it for the time indicated on the package. Shape the boiled barley into small discs about 3/4 inch (2 cm) thick, using a cookie cutter. Season with salt and unfiltered extra-virgin olive oil.

Cut the cabbage into very fine strips, season with extra-virgin olive oil, white wine vinegar, salt, and cumin ground in a coffee grinder. Place small mounds of the sliced, seasoned cabbage on the plates. Cut the ham into thin slices and arrange it on the cabbage with the barley to form petals.

AMBERJACK FILLET
COOKED IN BELGIAN ALE
WITH YOUNG STEAMED VEGETABLES

SERVES 4

1 AMBERJACK WEIGHING 1 1/2 POUNDS (700 G)
2 CUPS (500 ML) BELGIAN ALE
4 FRESH ZUCCHINIS
4 FRESH CARROTS
1 BUNCH OF FRESH HOPS
EXTRA-VIRGIN OLIVE OIL
SALT AND PEPPER

PREPARATION

Begin by filleting the amberjack, carefully removing any tiny bones with tweezers. Use a flexible knife to remove the skin and cut the fillets into portions for 4 servings.

Next, bring the Belgian ale to a boil, then turn off the heat and let it sit for 5 minutes. Submerge the amberjack fillets in the beer and let them soak for 8 minutes. Drain them carefully to prevent any breakage.

While the amberjack is infusing with the beer, clean and wash the vegetables. Using a mandolin, slice them into thin 1/10-inch (2 mm) thick rounds. Steam the vegetables for 4 minutes until tender, then season them with olive oil, salt, and pepper.

To serve, arrange the colorful vegetable slices on plates, alternating them, and place the amberjack fillets on top. Serve this dish at room temperature.

PAIRING BEER AND FOOD

TUNA-RABBIT
WITH SEASONAL VEGETABLES
AND GELATIN WITH PILS

SERVES 4

4 RABBIT LEGS
1 ZUCCHINI
1 FENNEL BULB
1/2 RED BELL PEPPER AND 1/2 YELLOW BELL PEPPER
2 STALKS CELERY
1 CARROT
2 WHITE ONIONS
4 FLAT BEAN PODS
1 BUNCH FRESH TARRAGON
8 GELATIN LEAVES
4 CUPS (1 LITER) OF PILS
1 BUNCH OF FRESH CURLY-LEAFED PARSLEY
EXTRA-VIRGIN OLIVE OIL
RED WINE VINEGAR
SALT AND PEPPER

PREPARATION

Brown the rabbit legs after seasoning them with salt and pepper. Dice the carrot, one stick of celery, and one onion. Brown them in a high-sided baking dish. Add the rabbit legs to the vegetable mixture, mix in half of the butter, and bake covered at 300°F (150°C) for about one and a half hours.

Meanwhile, clean, wash, and cut the remaining vegetables into lozenges 3/4 to 1 1/4 inches (2 to 3 cm) long. Cook the vegetables separately, browning them in a little extra-virgin olive oil over high heat. Immediately afterward, add a small amount of water and continue cooking until it has almost completely evaporated. Once the cooking is finished, remove the rabbit legs from the pan, wait for a few minutes, and then remove the meat from the bone, shredding it. Combine the vegetables with the rabbit meat and strain the cooking water into a pan. Add the remaining beer and the leaves of gelatin previously softened in cold water. Stir until the gelatin is completely dissolved. Pour the liquid into the dish with the shredded meat and vegetables. Cover with food-grade plastic wrap, ensuring it is in contact with the meat and vegetables to create an even surface. Allow it to rest in the refrigerator for at least one hour. Chop the tarragon and parsley separately. Season and finish the gelatin with extra-virgin olive oil, salt, pepper, parsley, tarragon, and a little red wine vinegar. Serve at room temperature.

COTECHINO SAUSAGE COOKED IN SMOKED BEER WITH SEASONAL VEGETABLES IN SWEET AND SOUR SAUCE

SERVES 4

5 1/4 OUNCES (150 G) NEW WHITE ONIONS
5 1/4 OUNCES (150 G) FENNEL
5 1/4 OUNCES (150 G) RED BELL PEPPERS
5 1/4 OUNCES (150 G) YELLOW BELL PEPPERS
5 1/4 OUNCES (150 G) CAULIFLOWER
5 1/4 OUNCES (150 G) CARROTS
2 CUPS (400 G) SUGAR
4 CUPS (1 LITER) WHITE WINE VINEGAR
2 TABLESPOONS (40 G) SALT
12 OUNCES (380 G) COTECHINO SAUSAGES
4 CUPS (1 LITER) SMOKED BEER

PREPARATION

Begin by bringing the beer and 8 cups (2 liters) of water to a boil. Immerse the cotechino sausages and cook for one and a half hours.

Meanwhile, clean the vegetables, wash them, and cut them into cubes. Then cook them in the vinegar with the sugar and salt, reducing until the vinegar reaches the consistency of a sleek syrup, but not as thick as honey.

When the sausages are cooked, cut them into pieces 1 1/4 inches (3 cm) thick and remove the skin. Serve by placing the pieces of sausage on top of the vegetables.

TRIPEL ALE RISOTTO

SERVES 4

14 OUNCES (400 G) VIALONE NANO RICE
7 OUNCES (200 G) PARMIGIANO REGGIANO
6 TABLESPOONS (90 G) BUTTER
8 CUPS (2 LITERS) TRIPEL ALE
1 BUNCH RADISH SHOOTS
EXTRA-VIRGIN OLIVE OIL
SALT AND PEPPER

PREPARATION

Begin by boiling the ale in a pan and removing 3/4 cup + 2 tablespoons (200 ml) from it.

Next, cook the Vialone Nano rice in extra-virgin olive oil and add salt. When the grains are very hot to the touch, start cooking the rice with the Tripel Ale and continue to cook for 12 minutes, stirring the rice occasionally.

Once the rice is cooked, add the butter, Parmigiano Reggiano, a few grinds of pepper, and the ale that was previously removed. Continue to cook the rice, stirring until it becomes creamy and soft.

Wash the radish shoots in cold water and trim them from the radishes using a small pair of scissors. Serve the risotto on plates, garnished with a few radish shoots.

STOUT SPAGHETTI
WITH A REDUCTION OF SHRIMPS

SERVES 4

3 CUPS (500 G) DURUM WHEAT SEMOLINA FLOUR
3/4 CUP (180 ML) STOUT
1 TEASPOON (4 ML) COGNAC
3 POUNDS 5 OUNCES (1.5 KG) RAW SHRIMPS
1 ONION
2 TABLESPOONS (20 G) TOMATO PASTE
3/4 CUP+5 TABLESPOONS (200 ML) WHITE WINE
1 STICK CELERY
1 CLOVE GARLIC
1 BUNCH FRESH OREGANO

PREPARATION

To prepare the pasta, mix the flour and beer in a bowl to create a moist, uneven mixture. Pass the mixture through a fresh pasta machine and create spaghetti, cutting them to a length of 6 inches (15 cm). If a pasta machine is not available, you can use ready-made spaghetti and cook them in a mixture of water and beer (4 cups/1 liter beer and the remaining in water).

Clean the shrimps by removing the shells and heads. Place the remaining parts of the shrimp in a pan with a small amount of oil, along with the onion, an unpeeled clove of garlic, celery, tomato paste, and cognac. Cover with cold water and simmer over very low heat until the liquid is reduced by two-thirds. Strain the sauce into another pan through a very fine sieve.

Cook the spaghetti, cut the shrimps into pieces, and once the pasta is cooked, toss it with the reduction, the raw shrimps, and the extra-virgin olive oil. Serve the dish, garnishing it with fresh oregano leaves.

LITTLE RED POTATO GNOCCHI WITH BARLEY MALT IN FISH STOCK WITH SHOOTS

SERVES 4

4 POUNDS 6 OUNCES (2 KG) RED POTATOES
3 EGG YOLKS
2 1/2 OUNCES (70 G) BARLEY MALT
3 TEASPOONS (20 G) SALT
2 1/2 OUNCES (70 G) PARMIGIANO REGGIANO, GRATED
2 1/2 CUPS (300 G) PLAIN TYPE 0 OR ALL-PURPOSE FLOUR
2 POUNDS 3 OUNCES (1 KG) CLAMS
2 POUNDS 3 OUNCES (1 KG) MUSSELS
1 POUNDS 2 OUNCES (500 G) COCKLES
1 SEA BREAM, ABOUT 11 1/2 OUNCES (330 G)
1 BUNCH PARSLEY
1 BOWL MIXED SPROUTS
3/4 CUP+5 TABLESPOONS WHITE WINE
3 1/2 OUNCES (100 G) TOMATO PASSATA
EXTRA-VIRGIN OLIVE OIL
SALT AND PEPPER

PREPARATION

Boil the potatoes in their skins. Meanwhile, prepare the egg yolks, salt, Parmigiano Reggiano, barley malt, and flour, keeping them separate. Once the potatoes have cooked, peel them quickly while they are still very hot, mash them with a potato masher on a work surface, and leave them to cool. To the potatoes, add the egg yolks, malt, salt, Parmigiano Reggiano, and finally the flour. Knead the mixture quickly so that it does not become wet, cut it into pieces, roll them on the surface to form long cylinders, then cut them into pieces about 3/4 inch (2 cm) long and roll them into dumplings. Place the dumplings on a tray covered with baking parchment and put them in the freezer, making sure they do not stick to each other.

For the broth, clean the sea bream. Soak the clams and cockles in salted water, remove the beards from the mussels. Fry all the mollusks in extra-virgin olive oil for 3 minutes with the parsley stalks, pour in the white wine, add the tomatoes and the whole sea bream, cover with cold water, and bring to a very gentle boil. Let it reduce by half and then filter it through a fine mesh strainer. Cook the gnocchi in salted water in another pot, drain, and serve directly on the plates. Cover with fish stock prepared earlier, a dash of raw extra-virgin olive oil, and finally the washed shoots.

PAIRING BEER AND FOOD

TAGLIATELLE WITH RABBIT RAGU IN AMERICAN PALE ALE AND SAUTEED HOPS

SERVES 4

4 CUPS (500 G) PLAIN TYPE 0 OR ALL-PURPOSE FLOUR
15 EGG YOLKS
1 STICK CELERY
1 CARROT
1 WHITE ONION
4 TABLESPOONS (40 G) TOMATO PASTE
1 POUND 2 OUNCES (500 G) RABBIT MEAT, CHOPPED
2 CUPS (500 G) AMERICAN PALE ALE
1 BUNCH FRESH HOPS
EXTRA-VIRGIN OLIVE OIL
SALT AND PEPPER

PREPARATION

For the pasta, pour the flour on a pastry board, add the egg yolks, and knead until the mixture is compact, smooth, and elastic. Cut the pasta into sheets and roll them out one by one with a rolling pin to make sheets about 1/25 inch (1 mm) thick. Roll out the sheets and cut them into strips no wider than 3/16 inch (5 mm). Form skeins with the tagliatelle just made and arrange them in a bowl sprinkled with flour, then put them in the refrigerator.

Wash and clean the hops, dry them, and put them in the refrigerator. Chop the onion, celery, and carrot, sweat in a pan with a little oil, add the meat, and continue browning. Then add the beer, the tomato puree, salt, and pepper, and cook for 1 hour.
Bring a pan of salted water to the boil, cook the tagliatelle for 3 minutes, and dress with the sauce.

Before serving, sauté the hops on high heat for 2 minutes in a pan with a little extra-virgin olive oil and salt, then add them to the finished dish.

ROUGHLY CUT PASTA WITH BARLEY MALT, WHIPPED CHEESE AND BALTIC PORTER

SERVES 4

4 CUPS (500 G) PLAIN TYPE 0 OR ALL-PURPOSE FLOUR
3 1/2 OUNCES (100 G) BARLEY MALT IN SYRUP
3 EGGS
7 OUNCES (200 G) CHEESE
1 1/3 CUPS (330 ML) BALTIC PORTER
SCANT 1/4 CUP (50 G) BUTTER
SALT AND PEPPER

PREPARATION

For the pasta, turn the flour onto a pastry board, then add the eggs and the malt syrup. Knead until the mixture is smooth, even, and compact. Cut the pasta into sheets and roll the pasta with a narrow rolling pin to a thickness of 1/25 inch (1 mm). Cut the sheets into irregular pieces, as the name of the pasta suggests.

Heat the butter in a casserole and add the beer, raising the heat to the maximum. With a rotary movement of the arm, mix the melted butter and the beer so that it forms a reduction. Put a pan of salted water on the heat and bring it to the boil. Then cook the pasta for 4 minutes, drain, then mix with the beer and butter emulsion. Plate it up, sprinkling it with the cheese grated earlier.

RAVIOLI ALLA FONDUTA AND DUBBEL JELLY WITH BUTTER AND SAGE

SERVES 4

2 1/2 CUPS (300 G) PLAIN TYPE 2 FLOUR
1 CUP (200 G) DURUM WHEAT SEMOLINA FLOUR
18 EGG YOLKS
10 1/2 OUNCES (300 G) FONTINA CHEESE
1 1/4 CUPS (300 ML) MILK
1 TEASPOON (5 G) AGAR AGAR
2 CUPS (500 ML) DUBBEL BEER
SCANT 1/2 CUP (100 G) BUTTER
SAGE
SALT AND PEPPER

PREPARATION

Infuse the Fontina cheese, cut into dice, in a bowl of milk for at least 2 hours. Afterward, dissolve the cheese in a double boiler, stirring the mixture. Use an immersion blender to make it smooth and even. Put it in a plastic bag and let it cool. Once it is cool, it should be compact.

Put the beer in a casserole, add the agar-agar, and whisk it while cold. Place the casserole on the heat and continue to mix until the beer comes to a boil. Then remove it immediately from the heat. Cool it well in the refrigerator, then blend the gelatin with the immersion blender to make a homogeneous cream with the same consistency as jam. Put the mixture in a plastic bag and refrigerate it.

For the pasta, mix the two flours and arrange them on a pastry board in a mound. Add the egg yolks and mix until it is compact, elastic, and smooth. Cut the pasta into sheets and roll it out with a fine rolling pin until it is 1/25 inch (1 mm) thick. Then arrange little knobs of beer gelatin and cheese on the sheet. Cover with another sheet of pasta and seal the two layers together by moistening them. Cut the pasta with a pastry wheel to make ravioli. Cook for 4 minutes in salted water, then stir them into the butter, which should already be salted and melted in the bowl in which you have browned the sage.

Serve very hot on a flat dish.

RECOMMENDED PAIRING: HELL

GRIDDLED SQUID WITH A REDUCTION OF HELL AND SUGAR-SNAP PEAS WITH BEER VINAIGRETTE

SERVES 4

4 SQUID, ABOUT 7 OUNCES (200 G) EACH
14 OUNCES (400 G) SUGAR-SNAP PEAS
1/3 CUP (100 ML) HELL BEER
1/3 CUP (100 ML) EXTRA-VIRGIN OLIVE OIL
4 TEASPOONS (20 ML) RED WINE VINEGAR
3 TEASPOONS (7 G) TAPIOCA FLOUR
SALT AND PEPPER

PREPARATION

Put the beer in a pan with the tapioca flour. Bring it to a boil on gentle heat and stir continually with a whisk until the mixture thickens. Cool it in the refrigerator. Use an immersion blender to emulsify the oil, the cooled beer mixture, salt, pepper, and vinegar to make a vinaigrette. Add the sugar-snap peas blanched in salted water for 4 minutes.

Cut the squid in half. Remove the skin and entrails. Cut slits in the flesh with a knife, creating a grid of lines at right angles to each other, while being careful not to cut through the flesh entirely. This process makes the squid soft and crisp at the same time. Wash and dry the squid, then add salt and season the squid with oil. Cook it on a hot griddle for 5 to 7 minutes.

Serve the squid with the sugar-snap peas, decorating the dish with a few drops of the vinaigrette.

PAIRING BEER AND FOOD

ROAST POUSSIN WITH INDIA PALE ALE AND POTATOES STUFFED WITH PIQUANT SAUCE

SERVES 4

4 POUSSINS, 1 POUND 2 OUNCES (500 G) EACH
2 CUPS (500 ML) INDIA PALE ALE
1 POUND 5 OUNCES (600 G) POTATOES
3 1/2 OUNCES (100 G) FRESH TOMATOES
1 OUNCES (30 G) SPICY RED CHILI PEPPER, FRESH
1 BUNCH CHERVIL
3 EGGS
ROSEMARY
EXTRA-VIRGIN OLIVE OIL
BAY LEAF
THYME
SALT AND PEPPER

PREPARATION

Season the poussins with salt and pepper, then immerse them in the beer with the aromatic herbs. Let them marinate for at least 10 minutes. Drain the poussins and dry them, then sauté them in a little oil in a non-stick pan. Transfer the pan into the oven preheated to 375 °F (190 °C), basting them with the beer marinade previously brought to the boil. Cook for 35 minutes. In the meantime, wash and clean the peppers, cut them into pieces, and beat them with olive oil and salt until creamy. Brown them in a pan for 4 minutes, then add the tomatoes, washed and cut into pieces, and season with salt. Cook until the sauce is reduced. Boil the potatoes in their skins in salted water. When cooked, peel them quickly and mash them in a bowl with a potato masher. Then add the egg yolks and mix, seasoning the mixture. Add the whites whipped to snow, gently folding them in, and pour the mixture onto a baking sheet lined with a sheet of parchment paper. With your hands lightly greased with oil, spread out the mixture to a thickness of 3/16 inch (5 mm). Cook in the oven at 350 °F (180 °C) for 15 minutes. Take out the soft potato biscuit and cut it into 3-inch (8-centimeter) squares. Spread them with the spicy sauce and form them into lasagnette (wide ribbon noodles), overlapping them. Garnish with rosemary leaves. Serve the poussins with the potatoes, garnishing with thyme leaves.

GLAZED PORK KNUCKLE WITH SMALL RED FRUITS, RASPBERRY BEER DROPS AND CREAMED POTATOES

SERVES 4

2 PORK KNUCKLES CUT IN HALF LENGTHWAYS
1 STICK CELERY
1 CARROT
1 WHITE ONION
1 1/4 CUPS (300 ML) WHITE WINE
1 BUNCH HERBS CONSISTING OF BAY LEAF, ROSEMARY, THYME, SAGE
1 BOWL RASPBERRIES
1 BOWL BLACKBERRIES
1 BOWL BLUEBERRIES
3/4 CUP+2 TABLESPOONS (200 ML) FRAMBOISE BEER
2 TABLESPOONS (5 G) TAPIOCA FLOUR
2 POUNDS 2 OUNCES (1 KG) YELLOW POTATOES
1 1/4 CUPS (300 ML) FRESH CREAM
3 TABLESPOONS (40 G) BUTTER
EXTRA-VIRGIN OLIVE OIL
SALT AND PEPPER

PREPARATION

Peel and wash the celery, carrot, and onion, cut them into cubes, and fry them in an ovenproof pan with olive oil and salt. Salt and pepper the pork knuckles, sauté them in a non-stick pan, pour in the white wine, add the red fruits after washing them, and bring to a boil. Pour the sauce over the knuckles in the pan, add the bouquet garni, and cook in the oven for 2 hours at 350 °F (180 °C). Put the beer in a saucepan, add the tapioca flour, and bring to a boil, stirring quickly with a whisk until it forms a thick sauce. Leave it to cool. Boil the potatoes in their skins in salted water. Drain and peel them, crush them in a pan, add the very cold butter, stir until it is well blended, add salt, add the cold cream, and transfer to the heat, stirring until you have a puree. Remove the knuckles from the oven, transfer to a serving dish, and then reduce the strained sauce until it is thick and glossy. Cover the knuckles with the sauce, add the mashed potatoes to the dish, and garnish with a few drops of the beer and tapioca sauce.

FILET OF RED MULLET WITH MASHED POTATOES AND BIÈRE BLANCHE WITH SPROUTS AND YOUNG LEAVES

SERVES 4

12 RED MULLET, ABOUT 3 1/2 OUNCES (100 G)
1 POUNDS 2 OUNCES (500 G) YELLOW POTATOESE
1 1/4 CUPS (300 ML) BIÈRE BLANCHE
1 BUNCH ARUGULA
1 BUNCH VALERIAN
1 BUNCH LOOSE-LEAF CURLY LETTUCE
1 BUNCH CASTELFRANCO RADICCHIO
1 BUNCH MIXED WILD LEAF SALAD
1 BUNCH ENDIVE
3/4 CUP+2 TABLESPOONS (200 ML) WHITE WINE
EXTRA-VIRGIN OLIVE OIL
SALT AND PEPPER

PREPARATION

Boil the potatoes in salted boiling water for 45 minutes.

Wash all the salad leaves in cold water, drain the excess water, place them in a container, and put them in the refrigerator. Fillet and bone the mullet. Keep them in the refrigerator until ready to use, covered with a moistened paper towel.

Once the potatoes are cooked, drain and peel them and put them in a blender, add the beer, salt, extra virgin olive oil, and blend until creamy. Heat a non-stick pan greased with olive oil, and sauté the red mullet fillets, which have been already salted, along with a part of the skin. After 2 minutes of browning, pour in the white wine. Let the wine reduce until it becomes creamy.

Pour the potato cream into a shallow dish, forming a layer 3/8 in (1 cm) thick. Add the salad greens dressed with extra virgin olive oil and salt, and finally, the red mullet fillets with the sauce in which they were cooked.

LAMB IN A HERB CRUST WITH A LAGER REDUCTION AND CREAM OF CHARD

SERVES 4

2 RACKS OF LAMB
1 BUNCH PARSLEY, THYME, ROSEMARY
SCANT 1/2 CUP (100 G) BUTTER
3 1/2 OUNCES (100 G) BREADCRUMBS
3/4 CUP+2 TABLESPOONS (200 ML) LAGER BEER
2 TABLESPOONS (5 G) TAPIOCA FLOUR
14 OUNCES (400 G) CHARD
2 TABLESPOONS (4 G) AGAR AGAR
EXTRA-VIRGIN OLIVE OIL
SALT AND PEPPER

PREPARATION

Combine the breadcrumbs with the butter, herb leaves, and a pinch of salt to create a thick, slightly grainy mixture. Compact it with your hands and place it between two sheets of parchment paper. Roll it out with a rolling pin until the herb crust is 1/8 inch (3 mm) thick. Refrigerate it to firm up.

In a non-stick pan, brown the racks of lamb that have been seasoned with salt and pepper. Allow them to rest on a baking sheet. Adhere the layers of the herb crust to the racks of lamb and bake for 12 minutes at 375 °F (190 °C).

Wash the chard, blanch it in salted water for 2 minutes, then drain and let it cool in iced water. Squeeze out excess water, sprinkle with agar agar, and place it in a saucepan after passing the mixture through a medium-meshed sieve. Bring it to a boil, stirring with a whisk, then let it cool in the refrigerator to create a firm jelly. Blend it with an immersion blender until it reaches the consistency of a very smooth cream, and season it with salt.

Combine the beer and tapioca flour in a saucepan, bring it to a boil, stirring with a whisk until it thickens to a creamy consistency.

PANCETTA COOKED IN KÖLSCH WITH SAVOY CABBAGE SALAD AND A BARLEY MALT REDUCTION

SERVES 4

14 OUNCES (400 G) FRESH PANCETTA
1 SAVOY CABBAGE
2 OUNCES (50 G) BARLEY GRAINS
2 OUNCES (50 G) BARLEY MALT IN SYRUP
4 CUPS (1 LITER) KÖLSCH BEER
EXTRA-VIRGIN OLIVE OIL
WHITE WINE VINEGAR
SALT AND PEPPER

PREPARATION

Cut the pancetta into 4 pieces to form 4 cubes, season with salt and pepper, and brown them in a hot non-stick pan. Sear the meat on all sides and dip it in beer that has been previously heated in a saucepan. Cook over very low heat for 1 hour.

Meanwhile, boil the barley grains in 1 1/4 cups (300 ml) of salted water for 10 minutes, then add them to the cooking water along with the drained malted barley. Stir well and strain into another saucepan. Reduce the mixture on the stove until it thickens. Remove the pancetta from the beer and let it brown in the oven with the grill on for 5 minutes until the fat from the meat begins to sizzle but without letting it color.

Slice the cabbage into thin strips, wash and drain it. Toss it with extra-virgin olive oil, salt, pepper, and white wine vinegar. Coat the pancetta with the barley malt reduction and place it on top of the cabbage salad.

HOT CHOCOLATE PIE WITH IMPERIAL RUSSIAN STOUT AND A COATING OF 72% FINE CHOCOLATE

SERVES 4

3 1/2 OUNCES (100 G) BITTER CHOCOLATE POWDER
1 CUP (230 G) BUTTER
1 1/2 CUPS (300 G) SUGAR
4 EGGS
1 1/2 CUPS (200 G) PLAIN TYPE 0 OR ALL-PURPOSE FLOUR
1 1/4 CUPS (300 ML) IMPERIAL RUSSIAN STOUT (PEATY IF POSSIBLE)

FOR THE COVERING
12 OUNCES (350 G) 72% DARK CHOCOLATE (AT ROOM TEMPERATURE)

PREPARATION

For the cake, cream the butter with the sugar in a mixer with a whisk until well combined (at least 15 minutes). When the butter turns creamy white and incorporates air, add one egg at a time and beat until fully incorporated, continuing until all the eggs are mixed in. Then reduce the mixer's speed and add the sifted cocoa powder that has been previously passed through a fine mesh sieve, followed by the finely sieved flour. Finally, when the flour is well incorporated, slowly pour in the beer.

Grease some aluminum molds with butter and then coat the insides with sugar. Place each mold on an electronic kitchen scale and add 3 oz (80 g) of the batter to each mold. Arrange them on a tray and, one by one, gently tap the bottom of each mold to remove any air from the batter. Then refrigerate them.

Bake the cakes in a preheated oven at 375 °F (190 °C) for 12 minutes. Remove them from the oven and wait for 2 minutes before turning the cakes out of the molds. Place each cake in the center of a plate.

For the covering, use a pasta machine, set the rollers to a thickness of 1/12 inch (2 mm), and pass the chocolate mixture through it to create delicate sheets. Cover each cake with a sheet. It's advisable to work quickly so that the covering sheets don't melt too much when placed on the hot cakes.

PAIRING BEER AND FOOD

SOFT HAZELNUT COOKIES WITH BROWN ALE FOAM AND CRESS

SERVES 4

FOR THE COOKIES
2 EGGS
1 CUP (200 G) SUGAR
7 OUNCES (200 G) HAZELNUT PASTE
1 1/4 CUPS (160 G) FLOUR

FOR THE FOAM
2 CUPS (500 ML) BROWN ALE
1/3 OUNCES (8 G) LEAF GELATIN
1 CUP (100 G) CANE SUGAR
1 BUNCH FRESH WATERCRESS

PREPARATION

For the cookies, whisk the eggs and sugar with an electric mixer until the mixture becomes fluffy and light in color. Add the hazelnut paste and stir gently to avoid deflating the mixture. Finally, add the sifted flour and mix well. Line a medium-sized baking pan with parchment paper, grease it with butter, and pour in the mixture, spreading it to a thickness of 1 inch (25 mm). Bake in a preheated oven at 350 °F (180 °C) for 12 minutes. Remove from the oven, take out of the pan, and cut into rectangles. Allow them to cool at room temperature.

For the foam, melt 1/3 cup (100 ml) of beer and the cane sugar in a saucepan over heat. Add the gelatin leaves previously soaked in cold water and stir until fully dissolved. Then add the remaining beer and pour the mixture into a siphon with 2 nitrogen charges. Shake vigorously for at least 3 minutes and store it in the refrigerator.

Clean the watercress, wash, and dry it. To serve, place a cookie in the center of each plate. Spray the beer foam over the cookies and then garnish with watercress sprouts, adding a spicy note to the dish.

RASPBERRY SOUP, GOSE BEER GRANITA AND CARAMEL SAUCE

SERVES 4

FOR THE SOUP
1/3 CUP (100 ML) ACACIA HONEY
GRATED LEMON ZEST
6 CUPS FRESH RASPBERRIES

FOR THE BEER DROPS
3/4 CUP+2 TABLESPOONS (200 ML) GOSE BEER
1/2 CUP (100 G) SUGAR

FOR THE CARAMEL SAUCE
1 OUNCES (30 G) BARLEY MALT
1 1/2 CUPS (300 G) SUGAR
1 CUP (150 ML) WATER

PREPARATION

For the soup, wash the raspberries and carefully dry them with absorbent paper towels. Place them in a jug, add the honey and lemon zest, and then blend the mixture with an immersion blender. Strain the mixture through a fine-mesh sieve into another container to remove all the seeds, and then refrigerate it.

For the beer drops, boil the beer with the sugar and reduce it by two-thirds over low heat. Pour the mixture into a baking dish, place it in the freezer, and every 20 minutes (5 times in total), fluff it with a fork. This will give it the consistency of granita as it begins to solidify.

For the caramel sauce, combine a generous 2/3 cup (100 milliliters) of water, the sugar, and the barley malt in a bowl. Mix them together and bring to a boil until the sugar starts to brown. Remove it from the heat, let it rest for a few seconds, and then add the remaining water. Gently mix it and refrigerate for a few minutes.

When serving, divide the raspberry soup among 4 deep bowls, add the granita, and drizzle a few drops of caramel sauce onto the dish using a spoon.

AMERICAN LAGER AND MINT JELLY WITH STRAWBERRY AND GINGER SALSA

SERVES 4

FOR THE JELLY
2 1/2 CUPS (600 ML) AMERICAN LAGER
1 1/2 CUPS (300 G) CANE SUGAR
15 LEAVES GELATIN
5 1/4 OUNCES (150 G) FRESH MINT LEAVES

FOR THE SALSA
7 OUNCES (200 G) STRAWBERRIES
2/3 OUNCES (20 G) FRESH GINGER
1/2 CUP (100 G) SUGAR
LEMON ZEST

PREPARATION

For the jelly, place the gelatin leaves in cold water with some ice for 10 minutes. Heat half of the beer in a saucepan with the cane sugar and bring it to a boil. Turn off the heat, add the squeezed gelatin leaves, and let them dissolve. Then add the mint leaves and let them infuse for 20 minutes at room temperature. Add the remaining beer and mix.

Take small metal cups and arrange them on a baking sheet filled with ice and a bit of water. Pour the mixture into each cup to a level of about 3/4 inch (2 centimeters) and add a mint leaf vertically. Keep the mint leaf vertical until the gelatin has set, then add some finely chopped mint in julienne strips. Pour another 3/4 inch (2 cm) layer of the mixture and, once again, hold the mint leaf vertically so that it's not completely submerged in the gelatin. Place the cups in the refrigerator and let them cool for at least 2 hours. If possible, prepare the jelly the day before so that it reaches the right consistency.

For the strawberry and ginger salsa, blend the strawberries together with the sugar, ginger, and lime zest. Pass it through a fine sieve to remove the seeds.

Serve by placing a disk of salsa in the center of each plate. Remove the mint beer jelly from the molds and place it on top of the salsa.

BARLEY WINE ICE CREAM AND BARLEY MALT ICE CREAM WITH LIME

SERVES 4

FOR THE BEER ICE CREAM
14 OUNCES (400 G) CREAM
3/4 CUP+2 TABLESPOONS (200 ML)) MILK
1 1/2 CUPS (300 G) SUGAR
3 1/2 OUNCES (100 G) GLUCOSE
1 1/4 CUPS (300 ML) BARLEY WINE
1 LIME, VERY GREEN

FOR THE MALT ICE CREAM
10 1/2 OUNCES (300 G) FRESH CREAM
1 1/4 CUPS (300 ML) FRESH WHOLE MILK
1 CUP (200 G) SUGAR
2 OUNCES (50 G) WILDFLOWER HONEY
5 1/4 OUNCES (150 G) BARLEY MALT

PREPARATION

For the Barley Wine ice cream, boil the beer with the sugar and glucose until it reduces by half. Add the beer to the milk and heat it to 185 °F (85 °C). Combine the cream with the milk and let it cool in the refrigerator. Then transfer the ice cream base to the ice cream machine and churn it until it reaches the desired consistency and a temperature of 43 to 18 °F (-6 to -8 °C).

For the malt ice cream, heat the milk to 185 °F (85 °C) with the sugar, malt, and honey, stirring with a whisk. Allow it to become lukewarm, then add the fresh cream. Let it cool thoroughly and place it in the ice cream machine to churn until it achieves the right consistency.

Serve in small bowls and grate fresh lime zest over the top. If you want to add a final touch, consider garnishing with a few edible flowers like violets.

BOCK FOAM, CANDIED FRUIT AND SWEET FRIED PASTRY CASSATA STYLE

SERVES 4

FOR THE BEER FOAM
3/4 CUP+2 TABLESPOONS (200 ML)) BOCK
4 GELATIN LEAVES
2 OUNCES (50 G) BARLEY MALT
2 OUNCES (50 G) ACACIA HONEY
1/2 CUP (100 G) SUGAR

FOR THE FILLING
7 OUNCES (200 G) FRESH COW'S MILK RICOTTA
3 OUNCES (80 G) ACACIA HONEY

FOR THE SWEET FRIED PASTRY
3 CUPS (400 G) FLOUR
1/3 CUP (80 G) BUTTER
2 OUNCES (50 G) GRANULATED SUGAR
2 EGGS
1 EGG WHITE
1/3 OUNCES (10 G) BITTER CHOCOLATE
2 OUNCES (50 G) MARSALA
4 TABLESPOONS (40 ML) WHITE WINE VINEGAR
4 CUPS (1 LITER) CORN OIL FOR FRYING
7 OUNCES (200 G) MIXED CANDIED FRUIT

PREPARATION

For the pastry, use an electric whisk to combine sugar and butter into a foamy mixture. Add one egg at a time, followed by the egg whites, bitter chocolate, and flour, ensuring all ingredients are thoroughly mixed. Then, add vinegar and Marsala, and roll out the mixture into sheets about 1/16 inch (1.5 millimeters) thick. Cut out discs using a round cookie cutter, wrap them around metal cannoli tubes, and fry for 1 minute in preheated corn oil. Drain, let them cool, and slide them off the cylinders.

Dice the candied fruit into small pieces and keep them in a refrigerator.

For the beer foam, soften the gelatin in cold water. Bring the bock to a boil with sugar, honey, and barley malt. Then, squeeze out the gelatin and dissolve it in the beer mixture. Stir well with a whisk and transfer the mixture to a siphon with 1 nitrogen cartridge. Let it rest in the refrigerator for at least one hour.

Combine the cold ricotta and honey, mixing them thoroughly, and refrigerate.

Remove the siphon from the refrigerator, shake it, and fill one end of the cannoli with foam and the other with the ricotta-honey mixture. Finally, sprinkle with diced candied fruits for decoration.

GLOSSARY

ACETIC: A descriptor for aromatic beers with hints and nuances reminiscent of vinegar. Positive and desirable in some cases (in sour beers or those matured in barrels) but unacceptable in all others.

ALCOHOL: One of the products of fermentation.

ALE: Top-fermented beer.

ALFA ACIDS: These are expressed numerically and together they represent the bitter substances in hops. The higher the value, the greater the bittering power of the hops.

AMILASES (ALFA AND BETA): The enzymes that, in mashing, break down the long chains of complex starch sugars into simple sugars.

BARLEY: The cereal that, once malted, is the main ingredient of beer.

BARLEY MALT: Barley that has undergone the malting process.

BEER: A generic term for any type of beer.

BODY: A characteristic of the finished beer, and more particularly an element of gustatory evaluation. It ranges from "watery" to "viscous" and depends on the unfermented residual sugar (dextrin) and other substances.

BOILING: The phase of the production process in which the wort is boiled, and the hops are added.

BREWING: The entire "hot" process in which the wort is created and will be fermented after it has cooled.

BREW PUB: A pub that produces its own beer, which it offers to its clients but does not sell commercially outside.

CARBON DIOXIDE, CO_2: Gas produced by yeast during fermentation and secondary fermentation in the bottle.

CEREALS: Plants whose fruits or seeds are rich in starch and are therefore used for fermenting.

COLOR (of beer): This may be derived exclusively from the types of malts used or, in some cases, by special ingredients added, such as fruit, for example.

DIACETYL: A molecule produced during fermentation that provides "buttery" notes. In some ales, it is acceptable at low levels, but it is not welcome in lagers.

DMS: Dimethyl sulfide, an aromatic molecule reminiscent of boiled corn. It is almost always a defect.

DRY-HOPPING: A flavoring technique that consists of adding hops to the fermentation vessel after fermentation has finished or into barrels.

ESTERS: Agreeable aromatic compounds in the "fruity" category. They arise from the combination and reaction of various substances in the production process, particularly yeast and alcohol, depending on the fermentation temperature.

FERMENTATION: The process by which yeast converts the wort into beer. The sugars are metabolized by the yeast, which mainly produces alcohol and carbon dioxide, along with numerous by-products.

FILTRATION: A phase of the preparation of beer in which the mash liquid is separated from the solid parts of the cereal grains (spent grains).

GERMINATION: An important stage of malting in which the seeds of the cereal are allowed to germinate to activate their enzymatic potential.

GRUIT (OR GRUYT): A collection of herbs, leaves, roots, and various essences that, until the 17th century, were used for bittering and flavoring beer before the introduction of hops.

HOP: A dioecious perennial climber that can reach a height of 20 to 26 feet (6 to 8 meters). The female flowers are rich in resinous substances and essential oils, and they are used to give the beer its bitter taste and enrich its aromas.

IBU (International Bitterness Unit): The measure of bitterness derived from hops.

IMPERIAL: An adjective generally used to emphasize a more "rich and powerful" version of a certain style. For example, Imperial IPA, Imperial Stout, Imperial Pils, etc.

LAGER: Bottom-fermented beer.

LAMBIC: A spontaneously fermented beer characteristic of Belgium, that is sour, complex, and suitable for aging.

LUPULIN: The aromatic oils and resins of hops.

MALTING: The process by which cereal grains are soaked, germinated, and then dried or caramelized or toasted.

MASHING: The preparatory phase of beer making during which the sugary wort is produced. A mixture of water and malted milled cereals is "brewed" at a particular temperature to activate the enzymes.

OXIDATION: The set of chemical reactions caused by the presence of an excess of oxygen in the finished beer or simply the result of aging or poor storage. Oxidized beer has the smell of wet cardboard.

PASTEURIZATION: The thermal process that beer may undergo to eliminate any micro-organisms. It is widespread among large industrial brewers but frowned upon by small micro-breweries.

PHENOLS: A family of aromatic phenolic compounds with fragrances ranging from medicinal to smoky, from cloves to tar.

RAW: An ambiguous term. It indicates an unpasteurized beer, but the beer is still produced by brewing the malted grain.

REINHEITSGEBOT: The Purity Law of beer. Dating from 1516 in Bavaria, it decreed that beers might only be made with water, malted barley, and hops (yeast had not yet been discovered).

SPARGING: The process of rinsing cereal grains with warm water to extract all the simple sugars produced.

SPENT GRAIN: The solid, insoluble part of the mashed cereal that must be removed before boiling.

STYLE (of beer): The objective and measurable data that define a particular type of beer.

YEAST: A single-celled organism of the *Saccharomyces* family that is responsible for the fermentation of the beer and, therefore, for the alcohol and carbon dioxide present in it.

AUTHORS AND PHOTOGRAPHER

FABIO PETRONI was born in Corinaldo, Ancona, in 1964. Currently, he lives and works in Milan. After studying photography, he has collaborated with some of the most renowned professionals in the field. His career has led him to specialize in portraits and still life, areas in which he has demonstrated an intuitive and precise style. Over the years, he has photographed prominent figures in the fields of culture, medicine, and the Italian economy. He collaborates with leading advertising agencies and has been responsible for numerous campaigns for major international clients and businesses. For White Star Publishers, he has published *Horses: Master Portraits* (2010), *Mutt's Life!* (2011), *Cocktails, Roses, and Super Cats* (2012), *Orchids*, *Tea Sommelier*, *Chili Pepper: Moments of Spicy Passion* (2013), and *Bonsai* (2014). He serves as the official photographer of the IJRC (International Jumping Riders Club) and is responsible for the visual aspects of its promotions dedicated to international equestrian competitions. Website: www.fabiopetronistudio.com

PETER FONTANA, born in 1971 in the Brianza region, is married to Federica (a non-drinker!), and they have three children: Arturo (named after the great brewing entrepreneur Arthur Guinness), Paolo, and Caterina. He ventured into the world of beer during adolescence, in provocative opposition to his friends who exclusively consumed wine. In 1990, on the eve of his final exams, he grappled with doubts about his future while sitting in an unassuming pub in front of a bottle of Trompe-la-Mort that he had never seen or tasted before. At that moment, he made a decision that would alter the course of his life: to collect beer bottles, specifically empty ones that had been consumed. During that time, Italy had limited offerings in this pursuit, but his horizons broadened as he traveled across Europe during his university years. Germany, Belgium, England, and Ireland became a bottomless wellspring from which to draw. The space in his room dedicated to collecting 100 bottles quickly reached capacity, and his fascination with the discovery of entirely new tastes and flavors only intensified his curiosity. In 1996, when the first artisanal micro-breweries opened in Italy, he eagerly embraced them, primarily as an opportunity to expand his bottle collection. His bedroom is now invaded by over 2,000 bottles, meticulously displayed in specialized racks with cupboards above. As his collection continues to grow, he reluctantly turned to boxes stacked in a cellar for storing empty bottles. However, as his passion for collecting appeared somewhat frivolous, he pursued other interests. He assumed the role of Borgrem the cleric during long evenings engaged in Dungeons & Dragons with friends. Then, at some point in the game, he acquired an abbey and initiated a brewery to support the inhabitants of his village: a seed was sown. This seed would sprout

later, in London in 1999, when he experienced a revelation: kits for brewing beer at home were available. He returned from England with a plastic fermenter concealed in his suitcase and his soiled clothes inside the fermenter. It was time to embark on his journey of brewing beer independently! He diligently studied numerous American websites on homebrewing since the practice was already widespread in the United States. He adapted a manual pasta machine into a miniature grain mill, crafted the required equipment, and acquired large saucepans. He set aside the can of malt extract that came with the kit from London. Then, with the company of his friends, he commenced brewing beer from raw materials: malted barley grains, hop flowers, and yeast. The result was an English Strong Ale with 8% alcohol—a love at first sip! From that point on, each month he embarked on experimenting with different ingredients and styles, involving friends and presenting the results at the initial competitions for Italian homebrewers. These competitions fostered comparisons and fueled his determination to excel. In 2008, he established the craft micro-brewery in Monza, of which he remains the owner and brewer: the *Piccolo Opificio Brassicolo del Carrobiolo - FERMENTUM*, a member of the Italian Union Birrai. Apart from producing highly sought-after beers using local ingredients and unique recipes, he organizes introductory courses for homebrewing and tasting sessions featuring quality beers. His beers and brewery have earned top accolades in the past three editions of the *Guida alle Birre d'Italia*, published by Slow Food Editore. In 2014, the brewery underwent expansion with a new production facility, including a brewpub (the first in his city), to provide numerous enthusiasts with the opportunity to savor his beers in the proper setting.

JOHN RUGGIERI was born in Bethlehem in 1984 but was raised in Piedmont. He received professional training in several acclaimed kitchens, including those of *Piazza Duomo* in Alba and *Scrigno del Duomo* in Trento. Currently, as the chef of *Refettorio Simplicitas*, an elegantly refined restaurant in the heart of Milan's Brera district, Ruggieri is dedicated to disseminating a newly rediscovered approach to food characterized by simplicity and a strong emphasis on the quality of raw materials. These ingredients are selected based on seasonality and authenticity. Ruggieri's culinary creations adhere to the most authentic traditions, incorporating many niche products indigenous to his region. His culinary style is characterized by simplicity, sobriety, balance, and, in its own way, almost ascetic.

ANDREA CAMASCHELLA, the editor and author of *Fermento Birra Magazine* and coordinator of the *Guida alle Birre d'Italia* published by Slow Food Editore, is a professor and judge in brewing competitions.

ALPHABETICAL INDEX OF STYLES

ALPHABETICAL INDEX OF NAMES

ALPHABETICAL INDEX OF RECIPE INGREDIENTS

PHOTO CREDITS

All the photographs are by Fabio Petroni except:
p. 1 Sergo/123RF; p. 14 Private Collection/Bridgeman Images; p. 17 G. Dagli Orti/De Agostini Picture Library;
p. 21 Private Collection/Photo © Liszt Collection/The Bridgeman Art Library; p. 24 Evgeny Karandaev/123RF;
pp. 30-31 belchonock/123RF; p. 155 bottom Dmitry Rukhlenko/123RF; p. 157 bottom andreahast/123RF

The authors would like to thank:

Andrea Camaschella and Michele Di Paola for monitoring the text.

Birra del Carrobiolo - P.O.B.C. Fermentum di Monza - for the beers and materials they made available.
Sherwood Pub of Nicorvo (Pavia, Italy) - Bere Buona Birra and Lambic Zoon of Milan for the props.

Originally Published by WhiteStar, s.r.l.
World English language edition by Mango Publishing Group, a division of Mango Media Inc.

Cover, Layout & Design: Dataworks

For permission requests, please contact the publisher at:

Mango Publishing Group
2850 Douglas Road, 2nd Floor
Coral Gables, FL 33134 USA
info@mango.bz

For special orders, quantity sales, course adoptions and corporate sales, please email the publisher at sales@mango.bz. For trade and wholesale sales, please contact Ingram Publisher Services at customer. service@ingramcontent.com or +1.800.509.4887.

Why We Love Beer: All You Need to Know About Beer History, Flavors, Types of Beer, and More

ISBN (pb) 978-1-68481-396-4 (hc) 978-1-68481-397-1 (e) 978-1-68481-398-8
LCCN: has been requested
BISAC: CKB007000, COOKING / Beverages / Alcoholic / Beer
Printed in the United States of America